GHOST SOLDIERS
of
Gettysburg

Searching for Evidence of Paranormal Phenomena on America's Most Hallowed, and Haunted, Ground

BY
JACK ROTH & PATRICK BURKE

Copyright 2011 by Cosmic Pantheon

COSMIC PANTHEON PRESS

PUBLISHED BY
COSMIC PANTHEON PRESS

www.cosmicpantheon.com

PROUDLY PRINTED IN THE USA!

THIS BOOK IS PART OF OUR PSI FIELD RESEARCH SERIES

Other books in the series:

Ultimate Ghost Hunter by Vince Wilson

Aliens Above, Ghosts Below by Dr. Barry Taff

Ghost Detective: Adventures of a Parapsychologist by Dr. Andrew Nichols

Parapsychology: Frontier Science Of The Mind by JB Rhine

Some of the names in this book have been changed in order to protect the privacy of the witnesses.

DEDICATION

Four score and seven years ago our fathers brought forth on this continent a new nation, conceived in Liberty, and dedicated to the proposition that all men are created equal.

Now we are engaged in a great civil war, testing whether that nation, or any nation, so conceived and so dedicated, can long endure. We are met on a great battle-field of that war. We have come to dedicate a portion of that field, as a final resting place for those who here gave their lives that that nation might live. It is altogether fitting and proper that we should do this.

But, in a larger sense, we can not dedicate — we can not consecrate — we can not hallow — this ground. The brave men, living and dead, who struggled here, have consecrated it, far above our poor power to add or detract. The world will little note, nor long remember what we say here, but it can never forget what they did here. It is for us the living, rather, to be dedicated here to the unfinished work which they who fought here have thus far so nobly advanced. It is rather for us to be here dedicated to the great task remaining before us — that from these honored dead we take increased devotion to that cause for which they gave the last full measure of devotion — that we here highly resolve that these dead shall not have died in vain — that this nation, under God, shall have a new birth of freedom — and that government of the people, by the people, for the people, shall not perish from the earth.

— *President Abraham Lincoln, speech delivered at the dedication of the Soldiers' National Cemetery in Gettysburg, Pa., on the afternoon of Thursday, November 19, 1863, four and a half months after the War.*

TABLE OF CONTENTS

ACKNOWLEDGMENTS

from Jack and Patrick

To my wonderful wife, Jean, for her ongoing support and belief in all that I do, you are the best part of my life! To my daughters, Emily and Shannon, who in their own right are becoming talented sensitives and paranormal investigators, you both are the light of my life. This book is also dedicated to my brother John, who has crossed the great beyond and is still telling me where to point the camera! To those other brave souls who have ventured forth with me on many a battlefield — Mike Hartness, Darryl Smith, Jack Roth, Mary Burke-Russell, Melody Hood Bussey, Terry Templaski, Richard Flaum, Susan Eshleman, Peggy Cole, Andrew Dodson, Harry Grant, Chris Carouthers, Karen Mitchell and so many others — this book is also for you. And for all of the men who gave their last full measure, regardless of which war or conflict, I thank you for your service!

Patrick K. Burke

I want to thank all of my friends and family members who have supported my research endeavors over the years. I also want to thank Dr. Andrew Nichols, who has not only been a true mentor to me, but a dear friend. This book is dedicated to my wife, Lisa, whose patience and understanding have allowed me to pursue my dreams with clarity of mind, and also to my son, Nathaniel, whose open-minded curiosity to all things mysterious constantly reminds me that searching for the truth is not only a worthwhile cause, but a freedom that is our birthright. And finally, to the brave individuals who fought at the Battle of Gettysburg, I honor your courage and sacrifice.

Jack T. Roth

MAP OF GETTYSBURG

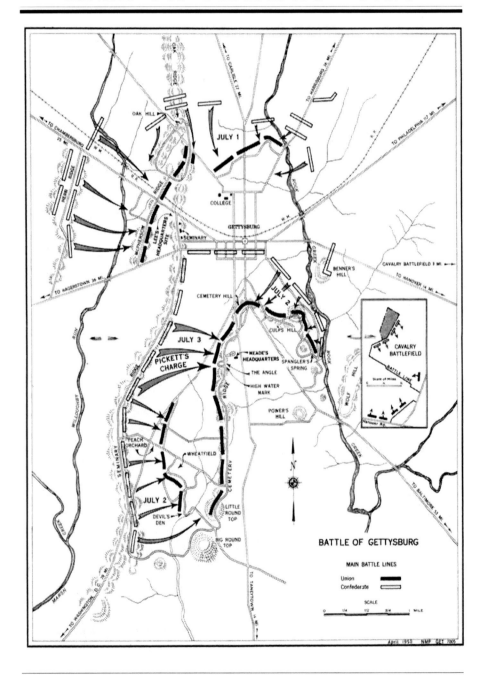

BATTLE OF GETTYSBURG

MAIN BATTLE LINES

Union
Confederate

SCALE

FOREWORD

by Dr. Andrew Nichols

Executive Director, American Institute of Parapsychology

Author of Ghost Detective: Adventures of a Parapsychologist

Military battles are among the most tragic and traumatizing of human events, and it is just such events that often result in the formation of a "haunted atmosphere." The battle of Gettysburg was certainly the bloodiest encounter of the American Civil War, and it is regarded as the turning point in the conflict that divided our nation. Thus, we should not be surprised that this battlefield in Pennsylvania has acquired a reputation for being one of the most haunted sites in the United States, if not the entire world.

Spiritualists believe that ghosts are earthbound spirits of dead people; that after death our spirits continue to exist in another dimension, but that some spirits — often in cases of sudden or violent death — become attached to a certain location where they can sometimes be seen, heard or felt by certain people. Evidence suggests that this explanation is inadequate for all or even many ghostly appearances. The majority of ghosts are almost certainly subjective; they have no objective reality outside the minds of those who experience them. Skeptics assert that all such experiences are hallucinations, dreams, or figments of the imagination, and that is the complete answer to the question of ghosts. Many reported apparitions can indeed be explained in this way, but it is not as simple as that.

The majority of parapsychologists, myself among them, believe that many ghosts are a type of telepathic image, created at some time during the past by a living mind during a period of extreme stress. Such a telepathic residue might remain for many years, available to anyone who is sufficiently endowed with the capacity for Extrasensory Perception (ESP). Research suggests that about 15 to 20 percent of the population is psychically sensitive enough to experience an apparition. This "psychic residue" theory is only that — a theory. As yet, it cannot be proved. It is a theory that could account for many ghosts, but certainly not all of them. However, it would also explain why most haunting apparitions seem to fade away after a number of years, as the telepathic image, like a depleted battery, gradually loses its "charge."

The honest answer to the question "what are ghosts?" is that we don't know. We do know that people experience ghosts. They can be seen, heard or felt by certain people. Methodical, responsible and honest ghost hunters can contribute much to our understanding of these mysterious phenomena, and with the help of dedicated researchers such as the authors of this book, I believe we will one day know what ghosts actually are and why they appear.

When I began my own investigations in the field of psychical research more than 35 years ago, ghost hunting was a pastime restricted to spiritualists, eccentrics, and a few isolated scholars. Today, a large number of serious, well-trained enthusiasts are actively engaged in the study of paranormal phenomena. My friend and colleague, Jack Roth, along with his co-author Patrick Burke, are among those who have established themselves as dedicated professional paranormal investigators.

I know Patrick through his fine reputation as a researcher and field investigator, and my friendship and professional relationship with Jack spans nearly two decades. Together, Jack and I have investigated numerous reports of hauntings over the years, and his dedication, enthusiasm and insight have been a source of inspiration for me. I can think of no one better suited to present the Ghost Soldiers™ of Gettysburg.

With this book, the two authors have provided us with a substantial contribution to psychical research; a study of one of the most intriguing and controversial of paranormal events — the ancient enigma of haunted battlefields. Whether or not you are already a believer in ghosts — or consider yourself a skeptic — no doubt you will be fascinated by this vivid and engaging account of their explorations on the frontiers of scientific knowledge.

INTRODUCTION

Since the dawn of primitive cultures, human beings have questioned what happens when they die. The idea of "spirit" goes back to early man, who became consciously aware of his mortality and wanted to know if getting mauled by a saber-toothed tiger represented his finite end. Consciousness gone. Kaput. Nothingness.

In 1871, England's first professor of anthropology, Edward Burnett Tylor, published Primitive Cultures. In it, Tylor explains the theory of "animism," which he defines as the belief in spiritual beings. According to Tylor, the belief in spirit began with early man's attempt to explain basic bodily and mental conditions such as sleeping, waking, trance or other unconscious states, dreams, illness and death. He believed that primitive man pondered on these things and developed the idea of a soul or spirit separate from the body, which was then extended to animals, plants, inanimate objects, heavenly bodies and deceased ancestors.

This led to primitive faiths, which in turn led to spiritual rituals. Some early cultures began to believe that the spirit wanders away from the body during periods of unconsciousness such as sleep, or that after death the spirit lingers near the body of the dead person. It was a common practice of groups holding such beliefs to pacify the ghosts of the dead by offering food, clothing and other objects these spirits might find useful in the afterlife. These types of rituals still exist in many cultures today. In fact, the practices of ancestor worship and the mourning rites of many modern civilizations most likely originated in this new found belief in the spirit world.

As civilizations and technology developed, however, it was no longer acceptable for people to simply believe in ghosts. Scientists and skeptics began to question how exactly it was that spirits existed, and of course, whether this could be proven scientifically. These inquiring minds focused on psychic phenomena, or psi, which refers to events that appear to contradict physical laws and suggest the ability to send or receive messages without the use of the five senses. These processes include extrasensory perception (ESP), the acquisition of information without using the known senses. ESP is comprised of telepathy, the transfer of information from one person to another without the mediation of any known channel of sensory communication; clairvoyance, the acquisition of information about places, objects, or events without the mediation of any of the known senses; and precognition, the acquisition of information about a future incident that couldn't be anticipated through any known related process. Along the same lines as precognition is retrocognition, the purported abstract transfer of information about a past occurrence. Another fascinating manifestation of psi is psychokinesis, which is the direct influence of mind on physical objects or events without the intervention of any known physical force.

The organized, scientific investigation of paranormal phenomena officially began with the founding of the Society for Psychical Research in London in 1882. It was the first organization established to examine these abnormal occurrences using scientific principles. In its early days, the SPR focused on the explosion of "extravagant paranormal claims … related to the spread of the new religion of Spiritualism." The American Society for Psychical Research was founded a short time later in 1885. Its mission has been "to explore extraordinary or as yet unexplained phenomena that have been called psychic or paranormal, and their implications for our understanding of consciousness, the universe, and the nature of existence."

In 1927, the pioneer of contemporary parapsychology, Joseph Banks Rhine, founded the parapsychology lab at Duke University and began his seminal extrasensory perception (ESP) experiments. He coined the word "parapsychology," the actual discipline that seeks to investigate the existence and causes of both psychic abilities and life after death using the scientific method. Due to Rhine's somewhat successful mental telepathy experiments, the great majority of psychical studies in the last 50 years have occurred in laboratories and focused on ESP. You see, in order for something to be deemed "scientific" and worthy of study in the scientific community, it must be observable, empirical, measurable and repeatable. Most metaphysical incidents don't comply with scientific protocols, but Rhine's experimental methods held the promise of supplying repeatable demonstrations. This has been a mixed blessing, because although psi research creates a pathway to understanding the human mind, the repetitive forced-choice procedures studied in laboratories fail to capture the kinds of ghostly experiences people report in everyday life. They also preclude consciousness-after-death possibilities.

This conundrum brings up the obvious question: How does ESP tie into ghostly encounters, if at all? Are ghosts manifestations of our psychic abilities, or can spirits of the dead (souls) actually manifest themselves in our earthly realm in tangible ways? Either way, the sobering truth remains that after more than 100 years of research conducted by some of the most brilliant minds on the planet, we're no closer to understanding the nature of spirit than did our saber-tooth-dodging brethren. However, in recent years, the growing number of paranormal researchers willing to actually leave the confines of the laboratory and venture out into the field where the real action occurs has yielded a strong body of evidence in favor of the existence of various types of ghostly peculiarities.

This book focuses on the field research my friend and colleague Patrick Burke and I have conducted on the Gettysburg battlefield. Our experiences support the idea that the best locations in which to collect evidence of ghostly activity are those where extreme violence and suffering has occurred. Unfortunately, the human tendency to search for spiritual enlightenment isn't the only thing that has prevailed since the dawn of primitive cultures; our inclination towards violence and conquering others shares in this dubious honor. As a result, a plethora of battlegrounds dot the surface of our planet. Nevertheless, if you're interested in ghosts and plan to visit a battlefield someday, you need to know what to look for. Before you can understand the nature of an experience, you must first ask an essential question: What exactly is a ghost?

One of the first things a paranormal field investigator learns is that a ghost isn't so simple to define. Many factors can cause a house or battleground to be haunted, and supernatural episodes are fairly diverse in nature. Wise men often declare that knowledge is power, and in the case of ghosts this is quite true. The best way to fight the fear of the unknown is to embrace and understand it. By properly discerning what you're dealing with, you'll be better equipped to confront it objectively, regardless of how scary it may seem on the surface. This is sage advice for paranormal researchers, who deal with potentially frightening situations all the time. Having said this, battlefield haunts tend to come in several guises.

Parapsychologists and researchers who remain open-minded enough to believe in such possibilities tend to define a ghost as an electromagnetic energy field containing a fragment of consciousness — or personality — of someone who has died tragically or traumatically. At the moment of death, the separation between the physical body and personality (soul) is hampered by a condition of emotional shock that prevents normal transition to the spirit world. As a result, the condition of death isn't recorded in the conscious mind of the one who has died. Life as it was continues to exist in the mind of the deceased, and the personality to whom this occurs is unable to recognize reality. This is referred to as a genuine, or intelligent, haunting.

Some parapsychologists believe genuine hauntings account only for a small percentage of ghostly phenomena and actually represent a telepathic connection between the minds of the deceased and the living witnesses. Physicality has been removed from the equation, so the witnesses aren't really seeing or hearing anything in a physical sense. This theory remains highly debatable, as finding the cause of this telepathic link still eludes the most ardent researchers.

An example of a genuine haunting might play out in this manner: You're touring a battlefield with your family when suddenly all of you notice a ragged, tired-looking man wearing a tattered uniform walking towards you. He stops, verbalizes how thirsty he is, and asks your son if he has any water. As your son reaches for his water bottle, the man suddenly vanishes. You all stand there, flabbergasted. The fact that this ghostly apparition acknowledged your presence and attempted to communicate with your son indicates that your family just interacted with a discarnate entity.

Location represents a major factor in determining who the intelligent entities might be in these cases. It has been theorized that spirits are connected to places through strong emotional bonds. In the above example, it can be surmised that this ghost soldier either can't or won't leave the theater of war due to the traumatic circumstances surrounding his death. He appears to be bound to that location by the emotional experience of the battle, and he's at least somewhat aware of his environment because he noticed your family and even asked for some water. By rule, if a certain location is shrouded in history — meaning notable happenings took place there — the more likely it will be haunted in some way. In other words, if you discover your home was once used as a makeshift hospital during a Revolutionary War battle or was the site of a double murder/suicide, don't be surprised if spectral energies abound.

Another type of spectral event is known as a residual, or imprint, haunting, which occurs when the energy from an emotional or traumatic event "imprints" itself onto the surrounding environment. Theoretically, energy can be absorbed by rock, brick, wood and concrete, as well as by trees, water and the atmosphere itself. These episodes, or snippets in time, replay themselves over and over again much like a broken record or looped videotape, occurring whenever conditions become favorable or when you walk into the area of occurrence and trigger the haunting episode. Identifying these "trigger" conditions — whether atmospheric, psychic or otherwise — remains a daunting, if not impossible, task.

Battle sites are conducive to residual hauntings. Fear, rage, despair, sorrow and other highly charged emotions flood an environment during the course of a battle. The battle ends, but these energies linger on, providing startling and sometimes life-changing experiences to those who are present when the replay occurs. Residual hauntings can be visual, auditory, olfactory and even gustatory in nature. The smell of sulfur, the sound of cannon fire and even the taste of blood represent fairly common types of aberrant battlefield experiences one might have on any given day.

The major difference between a genuine haunt and a residual haunt, besides the fact that a residual haunting doesn't involve the actual spirit of a deceased person, is that during an imprint playback, the same phenomenon occurs repeatedly with no changes in the action being witnessed. For example, you're visiting Gettysburg and see a bunch of reenactors performing regimental maneuvers near The Wheatfield. They march into the Rose Woods and seem to vanish into thin air. You track down a park ranger and describe to him what happened, and he informs you no reenactors were given permits to be on the battlefield that day. He also grins as if to say, "You're not the first person to see the 'phantom regiment,'" and you walk away shaking your head. If this exemplifies a residual haunting, your description of the incident should mirror other accounts given by different witnesses, regardless of when the encounter occurred.

After three days of fighting in Gettysburg, more than 51,00 men became casualties of war.

Another brand of high strangeness is known as an object haunting. Let's imagine you go to an antique store and buy an old locket. You bring it home, and within a week strange things start happening around your house. One of two possibilities exist in this scenario: 1) The intelligent consciousness of a deceased person, who was very attached to this locket while alive, follows you home with it.

One day you see the ghostly image of an elderly woman walking down your staircase. It startles the heck out of you. Guess what? Your house is now genuinely haunted because of the presence of this locket. You bring the locket back to the antique store, and the sightings cease; or 2) The emotional energies imprinted in the locket start to affect your mood. Unbeknownst to you, the person who wore this locket in 1926 was brutally murdered. You start feeling unnaturally sad or morose whenever you wear or are near the object. You begin to experience feelings of dread and even become more prone to violence. You're now experiencing a residual energy force directly related to the locket, and you learn the hard way that you're clairvoyant. You discard the locket and start to feel better immediately.

Combat zone object hauntings are usually associated with the personal objects that belonged to soldiers who died during a battle (e.g., diaries, photos, Bibles, guns, knives, lucky charms). The presence of these objects, now buried somewhere on the field or housed in the visitor center museum, can facilitate a psi experience and elicit strong emotional responses from visitors. The strong bonds associated with these objects can also enhance the prevalence of intelligent haunts. Let's suppose a soldier who fought at Little Round Top carried a tintype of his wife in his pocket. He was very suddenly and violently shot and killed in action. From time to time, his spirit is seen wandering around the base of Little Round Top, as if searching for something. He seems unaware of either time or his unfortunate circumstance (remember the phrases "fragment of consciousness" and "condition of emotional shock" used to define a ghost earlier in this chapter). The tintype actually was found and taken from the battlefield in 1867 by a looter, but the ghost soldier's strong connection to the photograph compels what's left of his consciousness to keep searching for it.

Although its existence is even more speculative than the more common aberrations mentioned above, portal hauntings represent another type of mysterious phenomenon that deserves mention here. Sometimes called energy vortices, portal hauntings are thought to be doorways to another world or dimension through which spirits can travel. Certain places seem to encompass a wide array of bizarre activity, including glowing balls of light, odd energy fields, strange shapes, and unexplained mists or fog. Some researchers believe these anomalies are traveling back and forth through a portal. The only evidence to support this comes in the form of high electromagnetic energy readings sometimes accompanied by a visual ripple or fluctuation in the surrounding atmosphere. The hypothetical existence of ley lines, or the alignment of a number of sacred ancient sites stretching across the planet, suggests that the Earth's natural electromagnetic energy fields often intersect at certain locations, making them prone to certain anomalies. In truth, we have experienced possible portal phenomena at Gettysburg more than once, and it appears the presence of these strong electromagnetic fields acts as a catalyst for preternatural occurrences. Timing these events, however, is difficult, and validation of the existence of these vortices isn't likely forthcoming anytime soon.

A mist forms by The Sach's Bridge.

The hauntings described here represent those most commonly experienced on battlefields. Other ghostly aspects such as poltergeists, doppelgangers, shadow people and elementals are all supported by various existential theories, but for the purposes of this book, they aren't often associated with battlefields and therefore won't be described in detail here.

Attempting to quantify these experiences, regardless of their nature, represents an important, yet difficult, endeavor. If we're ever going to gain a better understanding of the human mind and spirit, we need to diligently document witness testimony and carefully measure tangible evidence in the form of electromagnetic energy spikes, ion fluctuations, temperature changes and other anomalous readings in the environment. Capturing and documenting audio and visual phenomena in the form of photographs, video footage and tape/digital recordings greatly enhances the possibility of turning a large body of evidence into compelling proof of the existence of ghosts. And along the way, we can honor those who came before us and, if possible, help the ghost soldiers who are stuck within their own emotional quagmire to finally move on.

We assay to document our experiences in an attempt to capture what Patrick calls "living history," or the historic moment from the perspective of the participants. In the pages that follow, you'll share in these experiences and gain a better understanding of what it may have been like to fight at the Battle of Gettysburg, where thousands of brave individuals gave the last full measure of devotion. And maybe you'll discover that getting mauled by a saber-toothed tiger doesn't signify your ultimate demise after all.

— Jack Roth

PREFACE

When Jack and I first met, it was apparent that we would develop a wonderful working relationship and friendship. The success we have had — both separately and together — is due in great part to our approach to paranormal inquiry. Jack's background is pure research, and he is, by far, one of the most detailed and persistent researchers I've ever worked with. In the Forward, he successfully outlines the basics regarding the nature of hauntings; he also provides keen insight on the subject of parapsychology and how it relates to how we perceive field research.

What I'm going to share with you is the "psi" side of paranormal investigating, which includes how a sensitive reacts to paranormal activity and operates within a team. A sensitive is a person who can see, hear or feel the emotions of those who have passed on. In my first book, The Ultimate Guide to Battlefield Ghost Hunting (2011© Cosmic Pantheon Press), I shared the method of investigating I've developed over the years called The Intuitive Science Method (ISM) and discussed briefly how quantum physics — or what I like to call quantum paranormal as it specifically operates in the Zero Point Field (ZPF)— enhances the communication process with spirits. ISM incorporates sensitives into the investigative team structure by using their abilities to find "hot spots" of paranormal activity. In this way, they are able to help facilitate the gathering of paranormal data.

I'm going to suggest you read a book by Lynne McTaggert called The Field: The Quest for the Secret Force of the Universe. In this book, McTaggert takes readers into the world of quantum physics. She focuses on the theory that there's an underlying force connected to all living matter, or a spider-web of connectivity, if you will. The force she refers to is known as the Zero Point Field (see Chapter 8: Gettysburg's Quantum Quirks). The concept of a universal consciousness among all things isn't a new one. Native Americans have always believed that all things are related to each other — rocks, trees, animals, the snow that falls on a wolf's face; in essence, we are all linked. As a sensitive, I've been experimenting within the ZPF since 2008, and I've found that by connecting directly into it, I'm able to access a wealth of information from the past, present and sometimes even the future. In terms of using the field to facilitate an investigation, I've found — as have others I've trained in the ISM — that our ability to collect verifiable data validating a haunting is truly remarkable; we merely need to focus on the right things.

So, what is the benefit of having a sensitive on your team? I can best illustrate this by sharing a story of an investigation we did at the Civil War battlefield in Shiloh, Tenn. in 2004. During our daytime walkthrough of the battlefield, my brother John (a sensitive) picked up on a lot of activity in an area infamously known as the Hornet's Nest, which was the last line of defense for Union Gen. Ulysses S. Grant's forces on the first day of the battle. Earlier that morning, we had scouted another location called the Bloody Pond, which earned its name because the pond turned red with the blood of the wounded and dying men who were desperately trying to quench their thirst. At the time, I felt that the activity in this area was minimal and debated whether we should return again that night. But as I always say, ghosts aren't on our timetable. The truth is, you never know what might happen at any given location, no matter what your first impression might be.

On the way back to the hotel to get some food and rest before the evening investigation, John told us that the Hornet's Nest would be active. I agreed, but I asked him why he thought so, and he said, "I told them we would be back to visit them tonight." That got me thinking about how we — as sensitives — interact with spirits, and how we could take it beyond the basic exchange of data. Might we also be able to ask the ghost soldiers to do something for us?

I decided to conduct an experiment, one that I've done a number of times while investigating at Shiloh. The premise is simple: I communicate with a ghost soldier on one part of the battlefield, establish a bond, and then ask him to tell other soldiers to meet me on another part of the battlefield. After standing on the edge of the Hornet's Nest for a while, a Union soldier made contact with me. I pulled out my water bottle and silently asked him if he wanted a drink. As I did this, John walked up and said, "Yes." I must have given him a confused look, but I wanted to see if he had heard both my silent

GHOST SOLDIERS OF GETTYSBURG

question and the ghost soldier's reply. John smiled that crooked smile of his and said, "You asked him if he wanted a drink of water, and he said 'Yes, thank you.' Just pour it on the ground and see what happens."

As I poured the water, I heard a whispered, "much obliged" and realized that John heard it too. I immediately asked the soldier if he would tell any other comrades of his nearby to meet us at the "pond." I explained to him that if he told everyone at the Hornet's Nest to meet us in about one hour, they could share a bit of their personal story.

I left three investigators at the Hornet's Nest while four of us drove back to the Bloody Pond. When John and I stepped out of the car, we looked at each other and laughed. The air was electrified, and we could feel the highly charged spirit activity in the area. John immediately saw movement on the edge of the pond closest to us, and Darryl "Smitty" Smith grabbed his camcorder and followed us to that location. I could see my breath, and since cold spots are associated with paranormal activity, I knew this was going to get really interesting. The average temperature at the other locations that night was approximately 63°, but the temperature reading around me now was 44°. I walked over to the area where John had seen the movement of shadow figures. Turning to face the camera, I asked if any of the soldiers would like to join me for a picture. I felt a few energy signatures move across my chest, but they weren't strong enough for me to believe that my request at the Hornet's Nest had been followed or delivered.

One of the other investigators with us was standing nearby using a walkie-talkie. He said that the team at the Hornet's Nest was getting some activity on both the EMF detector and natural tri-field meter when they captured two possible spirit voices on their digital recorders. It was now 12:35 a.m., and based on what was going on at the Hornet's Nest I knew it was time to really stir up the energy. I called out to the ghost soldiers: "Hey, Boys! Ya'll going to give us something to talk about? I got to tell you that the boys at Gettysburg have always given us great pictures!"

John called out to the ghost soldiers just as I stopped talking: "How about a bunch of you fly around Patrick over there as if you've just come from the Hornet's Nest." Suddenly, I felt at least half a dozen energy signatures all around me. I asked Smitty if he was picking anything up on his equipment, and he responded, "Lots of energy signatures."

When it comes to quantum paranormal events like those I've described above, you'll have the best chance of capturing something if you have a sensitive on your team. Do you always capture evidence? No. But you will greatly increase your chances by 1) having a plan of action, 2) knowing the military and civilian history of the battle, and 3) approaching the ghost soldiers with respect. Keep in mind that these men — and sometimes women — sacrificed their lives for a cause they believed in enough to die for. When you're faced with a spirit attempting direct interaction, realize that — although they no longer have a corporeal body — they are still alive and deserve the respect that you would give to any other person you meet. And always ask permission to capture their picture or voice; it's a simple courtesy that goes a long way. And finally, when you're done, thank the ghost soldiers for interacting with you and remind them that they cannot follow anyone home, but that you will be back to visit them again.

Jack and I have a specific goal in mind with this book and other Ghost Soldiers™ books to come. We aspire to share the history of these great battles through the eyes of the participants — the ghost soldiers – who can provide a detailed knowledge of these historical events like nobody else. In order to accomplish this, we use every investigative method at our disposal and incorporate both known and theoretically scientific principles, as well as the benefits of our innate psi abilities. For without utilizing intuitive thought, we would be remiss in our approach to investigating phenomena that obviously transcend our tangible reality.

— Patrick Burke

CHAPTER 1 - THREE DAYS IN JULY

"In great deeds something abides. On great fields something stays. Forms change and pass; bodies disappear, but spirits linger, to consecrate ground for the vision-place of souls."

- Joshua Lawrence Chamberlain, speaking at the dedication of the monument to the 20th Maine, October 3, 1889, Gettysburg, PA

When I was 15, my mom and I spent the entire summer at our second home in St. Mary's County, Md. There wasn't a whole lot to do there, but a friend of my parents known to me as Col. Boyer, a venerable older gentleman who served through both World Wars, got a hold of me when he found out I was in town and asked if I could help unpack and organize some of his books, which were too heavy for him to heft around. So of course I agreed.

The Colonel's book collection was outstanding; every book you could imagine written on military history was there. During the second week of organizing, I came across a box that was tucked away in a corner. The books inside had that musty, haven't-been-read-in-a-long-time smell to them. I picked up the first book and discovered the wonderful world of Official Reports of the Battle of Gettysburg, and that summer I read the entire book of reports, which were written by Union and Confederate commanders who participated in the battle. I've been hooked on history — and especially military history — ever since.

Once I became interested in investigating haunting phenomena, I decided to follow my heart and focus on battlefields. There are several reasons for this. First and foremost, William Tecumseh Sherman, a well-remembered Union general, once stated simply, "War is hell." If you accept this description as accurate and apply it to certain theories associated with paranormal phenomena, then battlefields represent the most likely places on which to capture paranormal evidence due to the profoundly traumatic events associated with them. In a haunted house, you're usually dealing with strong emotions manifested by one or maybe dozens of people over several decades. On battlefields, unspeakable and horrific emotions emanated from thousands of men in a very short period of time. The bottom line, as Jack likes to say, is that "battlefields can't be matched from an emotional intensity standpoint, and as such they represent the best 'outdoor laboratories' paranormal investigators have at their disposal at which to conduct valuable field research."

Another reason, perhaps stemming from a deeper spiritual urge, is that I honestly feel drawn to these ghost soldiers. The heroic and unfortunate souls who sacrificed everything on battlefields across the globe have stories to tell, and I want to share these stories with others in honor of their sacrifices. When visiting battlefields, I often wonder to myself, "What was it like fighting on this particular spot for these boys?" and "What horrors did they endure while trying to act courageously and survive at the same time?" For whatever reason, I feel compelled to know these things ... maybe because we owe it to them in some way ... to understand, no matter how sad or painful that knowledge might be.

When Jack and I met at a conference some years ago, I knew immediately that a kindred spirit stood before me. We talked all day and into the wee hours of the morning with a group of friends and associates. It soon became apparent, as our mutual friend and researcher Melody Bussey pointed out, that Jack and I viewed the area of battlefield paranormal research from the same perspective. Add to that our mutual love of all things historic, and a fast friendship developed. I remember one of the first things Jack conveyed to me was that "attempting to communicate with ghost soldiers, as well as experiencing the strong residual energies associated with battlefields, gives us a unique and very rare opportunity to 'touch' history." These anomalies act as "time machines," he added, enabling us to transcend time and space in order to touch the past. I couldn't have agreed more.

We both strongly believe that we can capture — and validate with the help of science — a genuine historic moment in time. We also feel that we can more accurately predict when paranormal phenomena might manifest by amassing a library of data that includes details of the various conditions typically present before, during and after the anomalies occur. By studying the patterns associated with ghostly phenomena, we feel it will increase our chances of being at the right place at the right time — a luxury that field investigators don't normally enjoy right now.

Based on our experiences, we also believe that it is just as important to acknowledge the benefit of having "sensitives" (a.k.a. mediums) on the team. These are individuals with the ability to recognize potential hot spots — locations that are more prone to paranormal activity. This information can help field investigators determine where to set up equipment and focus their attention. By bringing along people who possess a heightened awareness of the spirit world — and who sometimes even have the ability to community with the spirits of the fallen soldiers — we have dramatically increased our capture rate in regards to paranormal activity. Our documented evidence includes photographs and video recordings of apparitions and shadow walkers, sound recordings of discarnate voices and battle sounds, and other strange anomalies.

Since that fateful meeting, Jack and I have embarked on a fascinating journey of exploration in an attempt to document and experience paranormal phenomena associated with battlefields. When we decided to join forces as researchers and began documenting what will ultimate lead to a series of books on ghost soldiers, we asked ourselves (and a few close friends) what battlefield we should focus on for our first book. The resounding answer was Gettysburg, and it came as no surprise.

The facts of the battle are simple: In June 1863, Gen. Robert E. Lee marched his Army of Northern Virginia into the Union stronghold of Pennsylvania and over the first three days of July, the Union Army of the Potomac met the Confederate invaders and defeated them at a small town called Gettysburg. It is seen as the great turning point in the Civil War. Most historians agree that from a strategic standpoint,

Gettysburg was the Confederacy's last chance at victory. By spring 1863, the Confederate task was becoming increasingly difficult. One of the reasons Lee invaded the North was to ease the strain on Southern resources. Almost the entire war had been fought on Southern soil, which had taken a financial and physical toll on the Confederate states. Lee hoped that by invading the North, he could ease that burden, and he also believed that another crushing Union defeat, especially on Northern soil, might force President

General Robert E. Lee

Abraham Lincoln to end the war and leave the Confederacy alone. Add to this the possible benefits a Confederate victory could have in persuading both Great Britain and France to recognize, and support, a new Southern nation, and the benefits seemed to outweigh the risks. In reality, however, the fate of the Confederacy hung in the balance.

Another factor in favor of making Gettysburg our focus was the enormity of the battle and the absolute devastation it inflicted on human life. In 1860, Gettysburg was a small town of about 2,400 citizens. For three hot, humid days in July 1863, two huge armies came crashing on top of them. Ninety-three thousand Union soldiers and 70,000 Confederates pounded into each other like two freight trains. The thought of 163,000 American soldiers having at each other in a town of 2,400 people is hard to imagine. When the fighting was over, approximately 53,000 of these soldiers were casualties. Of this number, 7,863 died in combat, 27,224 were wounded and of those wounded at least a quarter of them died from their wounds. Add to this 11,199 soldiers who were either captured or declared missing in action, and you're left with unimaginable carnage. This represented the largest number of casualties in any battle of an already-bloody war — a casualty rate of more than 31 percent! The total American population in 1863 was only 31 million, which makes the percentage of households affected by this one battle staggering by normal standards.

Gettysburg took on an even greater mythical quality when President Lincoln decided to accept an invitation to speak at the dedication of a cemetery for many of the soldiers killed in the battle. During this ceremony, Lincoln delivered his famous Gettysburg Address. His speech, considered one of the most brilliant by any statesman in history, resonated with hope and national unity at a time when people were numb from the death and destruction secession had brought. Lincoln's words read like poetry with phrases such as "conceived in liberty" and "all men are created equal." Perhaps the most stirring part resides in the words "that government of the people, by the people, for the people, shall not perish from the earth." Lincoln's brilliant speech made the battle even more significant historically, as both continue to define the broader, philosophical meaning of separation, suffering and reunion.

All of these factors add up to Gettysburg representing the perfect environment in which to conduct paranormal field research. The overwhelming number of documented paranormal experiences in Gettysburg suggests that, as Joshua Chamberlain eloquently suggested, something does stay and spirits do in fact linger. Even when we use critical, objective, scientific reasoning to discount the majority of these experiences as misinterpretations of normal events, a wealth of compelling, corroborative, verifiable evidence remains, including scientific data and video, still photographs, electronic sound recordings, and first- and second-hand eyewitness testimony from our investigations alone.

From a research standpoint, we always start with the history of the battle. By knowing everything about the regiments that fought in a particular area, we not only obtain a clearer picture of the events that took place, but we can also attempt to communicate with the ghost soldiers on a more intimate level. Our research takes us to the individual men in the company. By reading their diaries and the letters they sent home, we gain a better understanding of their everyday lives as soldiers, as well as the intimate details associated with their strongest emotions felt in the heat of battle.

We feel our methods are both respectful to the ghost soldiers and successful from an investigative standpoint. Our goal for this book is to share the evidence we've accumulated over the years in order to provide people with a better understanding of not only paranormal phenomena, but of the hardships and horrors tens of thousands of soldiers — many merely boys — experienced when they fought at Gettysburg for three days in July 1863. After all, they deserve to have their stories told.

— Patrick Burke

CHAPTER 2 ~
GETTYSBURG'S
RESIDUAL HAUNTINGS

"Things we do and experience have resonance. It can die away quickly or last a long time; it can have a clear center frequency or a high bandwidth; be loud, soft or ambiguous. The present is filled with past experience ringing in various ways and now is colored by this symphony of resonance."

- Paul Lansky, electronic music composer

*Are some soldiers doomed to repeat that fateful
weekend again and again?*

An important part of the paranormal research process is the documentation of experiencer testimony. In the world of parapsychology, "experiencer" is a fancy word for "eyewitness," or a person who has a first-hand encounter with the paranormal. During a group weekend investigation of Gettysburg, I interviewed several people who came along to learn how to conduct field investigations. As is almost always the case, many of them were there because they had experienced paranormal phenomena in the past and were hoping to learn more about what may have happened to them. One such gentleman named Brad was fascinated with the paranormal, but particularly as it applied to battlefields. I soon learned he had experienced several life-changing encounters at Gettysburg. He allowed me to document the following testimony:

In the summer of 1990 when I was 17 years old, my parents took me on a three-week summer vacation. We drove all over the eastern half of the country, and since Civil War history was one of my passions, we spent three days in Gettysburg. I also have a passion for ghosts and the supernatural, but I had no idea these two interests were going to come together during our visit there.

Ironically, we arrived at Gettysburg on July 1 and left on July 3, the actual dates of the battle in 1863. Perhaps the timing was perfect to be able to experience the encounters I had, but whatever the reason, the following two events occurred in front of my own eyes.

The first encounter was in the infamous Jenny Wade house. This is the home where the only civilian during the battle was killed. Apparently, Jenny Wade was baking bread for Union soldiers when a stray musket ball came through the front door and struck her in the back. The house still stands as it did in 1863 — with original windows, doors and floors, and still peppered with bullet holes. In fact, a wall upstairs still remains as a pile of bricks after a cannon ball blew through it, and the cannon ball still lies imbedded in part of the wall. I'm no psychic, nor do I claim to be, but the overall eerie feeling you get when you walk into this house is overwhelming, and a true sense of tragedy really falls upon you.

Keep in mind I had never heard about the Jenny Wade house, nor had I heard that many investigators believed it was haunted. If I had, I would never have gone in by myself. It was early in the morning on July 2, and while my parents ate breakfast at the hotel, I went down to get tickets for the tour of the house. The woman operating the tour told me I was more than an hour early for the tour but that I should feel free to go in and look around by myself. Armed with my video camera (I documented the whole trip), I went in. I started downstairs and viewed a film on the story of the day Jenny was killed, then headed upstairs. The stairs were original to the house and obviously very creaky. I viewed the upstairs, then headed back down a second set of stairs on the other side of the room.

When one walks with a video camera, it bounces back and forth. This is what was happening as I walked down the stairs. When I got to the bottom of the stairs, I stopped, the camera stopped bouncing, and I kept filming. Later, I watched the video, and from the top of the stairs, you could hear distinct heavy footsteps coming down behind me — several seconds after I stopped at the bottom! Had I known this was happening at the time, I would have split.

The next stop on my self-guided tour was the basement. This was where the family laid the body of Jenny Wade until the funeral. As I was walking out, all of the lights went off, and I smelled a pungent, sulfur-like odor. Just at that moment, a three-dimensional, lightly glowing haze appeared for about five seconds in the corner of the room. Five seconds seemed like an eternity as I sat there frozen with every hair standing up on my body. I DID split this time, with haste, and was too shaken up to tell the tour guide what happened.

My third encounter during my visit occurred on July 3 as we were leaving the battlefield. It was about 11 a.m. on a clear, very hot morning. As my parents and I drove through the battlefield park, I looked off to the area of a wheat field, where a particularly bloody skirmish took place during the battle. I noticed a regiment of about 30 Union soldiers marching in formation approximately 100 yards off the road heading towards a ridge. I told my dad to stop the car; I grabbed my video camera and started sprinting across the field to catch up with them.

Since we were there on the anniversary of the battle, I thought it was a reenactment group practicing some formation maneuvers. It seemed as if I couldn't catch up no matter how fast I ran. I stopped on *occasion and got some pretty good shots of them, but I noticed how silent they seemed to be. All you could hear was the wind rustling through the wheat. They headed over a ridge and out of site. I got to the top of the ridge about a minute later, looked around and saw nothing for miles over an empty valley. There wasn't a single soldier in sight. There's no way they could have gone anywhere else. Beyond the ridge is a vast, open countryside, and I was less than a minute behind them.*

When I got to a VCR, I popped in the tape, and sure enough, there were the soldiers as clear as day. I just knew I had a videotape with ghosts on it. Every time I show it to people, they don't believe me because the soldiers are as solid as real people on video, but I know what I saw (or didn't see) when I looked over the ridge. Several years later, I saw a TV show on the ghosts of Gettysburg, and one of the stories was about visiting Japanese dignitaries who pulled their limousine over to the side of the road and watched a regiment of Union soldiers march in formation several feet in front of them. They called the park rangers and thanked them for arranging the demonstration for them, but alas, there was no demonstration arranged or scheduled.

Several other people have seen a similar phantom regiment on the battlefield, and this particular phenomenon has come to be known as the Ghost Regiment of Gettysburg. I honestly believe this is what I saw; and whether people believe me or not, I know what I videotaped is the real thing.

Were Brad's experiences at Gettysburg chapters of the past unfolding themselves, and if so, to what purpose, and why to Brad? Brad's encounters, and many other documented paranormal experiences at Gettysburg, may represent what was described in the Introduction as residual hauntings, which theoretically occur when past events are somehow "imprinted" on environments and then experienced by eyewitnesses (via retrocognition) at a later time — sometimes even decades or centuries later. The imprint theory, as you may recall, proposes that environments with traumatic emotional histories — and specifically the physical elements that make them up such as rocks, trees, water sources, man-made dwellings, etc. — act as recording devices, somehow absorbing and then replaying events that those with a sixth sense or keen intuition — or who just happen to be in the right place at the right time — can experience via visual, auditory, olfactory and/or other sensory perceptions. Gettysburg would appear to be the perfect conduit for such activity, considering its traumatic emotional history and the large scale of such trauma (53,000 + casualties in three days of fighting). Did Brad witness a recording of a Union regiment marching in formation 127 years prior to his visual encounter? It appears more plausible than him seeing the actual spirits of 30 separate individuals still marching in formation. This event likely constitutes an activity that occurred when these soldiers were still alive, but that was replayed more than a century later for one reason or another.

Loyd Auerbach, director of the Office of Paranormal Investigations and author of numerous books on the paranormal, emphasizes that residual hauntings involve the recorded activity of the living, not the dead. "Although the subject(s) of the recording may be long dead, the activity was impressed upon the environment when they were alive," he explains. "This is analogous to videotaping a person doing something — you can't really do that when the person is dead. They kind of just lie there."

Residual hauntings are most commonly referred to as "place memory" by parapsychologists and academic researchers. In less formal circles it is called "cinema of time" and is often associated with Stone Tape Theory. Andrew Nichols, Ph.D., professor, author and founder of the American Institute of Parapsychology (AIP), points out that paranormal phenomena often share similar characteristics, which makes it difficult to create clear lines of distinction. For example, he says, a probable relationship exists between retrocognitive experiences and psychometry, or object reading, which is the ability to perceive information about the history and owners of an object as practiced by psychics. "In fact," he adds, "they are very likely to be very similar, if not identical, phenomenon."

Auerbach agrees that place memory seems to be an extension of psychometry. One interpretation is that the object — and what is a house but a big object — becomes a focal point for retrocognition. However, an alternative interpretation is that something about the object, building, battlefield, etc., essentially "records" information as it exists. "Human beings are capable of picking up on these environmental recordings and essentially play back bits of the information in their own perceptions/consciousness," he explains. "Most often, emotional events (or emotions themselves) are behind the more likely perceptions/recordings, although on occasion the recordings seem to be of very mundane activity."

To muddy the waters further, similar phenomena are also referred to as time slips or time warps, depending on the specific characteristics associated with them. It remains a highly debated topic within the paranormal research community, yet one that offers an incredible opportunity to learn a great deal not only about paranormal mysteries, but history itself. For example, in Brad's case, greater detail of the soldiers' uniforms may have provided researchers with an opportunity to corroborate the encounter from a historical standpoint. Could this have been an imprint haunting of Civil War soldiers marching at Gettysburg more than a century earlier? And if so, could Brad have provided researchers with details of the battle that historians could never piece together from ancient artifacts and/or the written record?

Brad's Gettysburg account isn't an isolated incident, as encounters with phantom ghost armies, discarnate soldiers and other elements from the past have been documented at length thanks to the dedication of paranormal researchers such as the late Andrew McKenzie. McKenzie, who was vice president of the Society for Psychical Research and author of numerous books on the paranormal, was a serious student of spontaneous cases in which protagonists fond themselves in surroundings that no longer existed. His task was not a simple one. Alan Gould, a colleague of McKenzie and former professor of Psychology at the University of Nottingham, professed that such cases are "fascinating, exceedingly rare and very hard to evaluate."

One thing McKenzie learned from his research was that characteristics associated with these phenomena are similar but not always the same, which raises the question of whether a past event has been imprinted on the environment for those with psychic sensitivities to experience at a later date, or whether some type of time slip has occurred, where a person, or group of people, travel through time via supernatural means.

Two respected schoolteachers, Charlotte Anne Elizabeth Moberly and Eleanor Frances Jourdain, had perhaps the most famous time slip experience ever recorded. While visiting the Palace at Versailles in 1901, they decided to go in search of the Petit Trianon, a small chateau located on the grounds of the palace. While walking through the grounds they both were impressed by a feeling of oppressive gloom. They claimed to have encountered — and interacted with — a number of people in old-fashioned attire whom they later assumed to have been members of the court of Marie Antoinette. In fact, at one point during this strange encounter, they saw who they thought might be Antoinette herself on the day in 1792 when she learned that the mob had stormed the Tuileries Palace.

In a widely publicized case from 1979, two English couples driving through France claimed to have stayed overnight at an old-fashioned hotel and decided on their return journey to stay at the same hotel but were unable to find it. Photographs taken during their stay, which were in the middle of the roll of film, were missing, even from the negative strips, when the pictures were developed.

One telling characteristic of these phenomena has to do with whether those experiencing them can take an active part in the event — interacting with the people and places being "visited." In the Versailles case, the two women were apparently seen, and spoken to, by people they saw. The English couples on holiday in France went further, staying in a hotel and eating dinner and breakfast in the course of their experience. Both of these incidents represent unusually prolonged events, taking place over at least several hours. These cases are more likely associated with some sort of time slip as opposed to a residual haunting, where the subject (e.g. Brad) is merely a passive observer of the past scene — one that plays out like a movie, imprinted on paranormal celluloid.

Another interesting element associated with these cases is an "altered state of reality" that's very difficult for the witnesses to describe. For example, many people report that, at the start of their experiences, their immediate surroundings take on an "oddly flat, underlit and lifeless appearance, and normal sounds seem muffled."

This surreal environment is sometimes accompanied by feelings of depression and unease.

In a case from Yorkshire, England, in the 1980s, an eyewitness described:

"What I remember is a brilliantly sunny day with lots of other people around, but as we made our way down, it just suddenly seemed as if no one else was there but my wife and me. An old woman appeared on the foot way opposite us. It became cooler and duller."

Another account includes an equally odd description of the environment, in which "the street seemed unusually quiet; there were sounds but they appeared quite muted." The witness also noticed that when she sat down, "the sun didn't seem as bright as it had been moments before." In fact, looking back years later, she described the light as similar to when the area had a partial solar eclipse.

Jenny Randles, a British author and former director of investigations with the British UFO Research Association (BUFORA), invented the phrase "Oz Factor" to describe this strange, seemingly altered state of being felt by witnesses of paranormal events. She defines the Oz Factor as:

"... the sensation of being isolated, or transported back from the real world into a different environmental framework ... where reality is but slightly different, as in the fairytale land of Oz."

Randle speculates that the Oz Factor points to consciousness as the focal point of these encounters.

I also experienced this Oz Factor just before hearing rebel yells in the Triangular Field at Gettysburg a few years ago (see Chapter 10: Echoes from the Past). I distinctly remember the atmosphere becoming very still and quiet just before hearing the shrieking "whoops" and "yips" that terrified Union soldiers years earlier. Oddly enough, I also remember thinking this is what it must feel like just before one goes missing in the Bermuda Triangle.

Could Brad have experienced the same phenomenon while chasing his phantom regiment at Gettysburg? Remember him describing how … *"I couldn't catch up no matter how fast I ran. I stopped on occasion and got some pretty good shots of them, but I noticed how silent they seemed to be. All you could hear was the wind rustling through the wheat."*

One thing is for certain, whatever Brad saw had a cathartic impact on his life. He, like so many others, experienced something truly bizarre at Gettysburg. Was he privy to a glimpse back into the past, or was he actually transported back in time for a few brief moments? And even more importantly, does Gettysburg act as a catalyst for such phenomena due to its history? If such a possibility exists, doesn't Gettysburg require our full attention as it applies to paranormal research and our quest to find the answers to these profound enigmas? I say "yes," as does Patrick, which is why we do what we do.

— Jack Roth

CHAPTER 3 - THERE'S THE DEVIL TO PAY

"We few, we happy few, we band of brothers;
For he today that sheds his blood with me
Shall be my brother."

- William Shakespeare, English
playwright and poet, from Henry V

Devil's Den is a maze of boulders and rocks that represents one of the most famous landmarks at Gettysburg. On the second day of the battle, this area saw fierce hand-to-hand fighting. Although historians and visitors alike focus mainly on the action in and around the Den, there's a modest elevation located at its northern end known as Houck's Ridge that saw the heaviest fighting of the day. The Confederate juggernaut had to fight through the Triangular Field, over the wall at the top of the field and then up this ridge in order to first get to the hazardous, jagged-edged ground of Devil's Den.

Capt. James E. Smith's 4th Battery, New York Light Artillery, consisting of three 20-pound parrot guns, was positioned towards the Triangular Field to aid the 124th New York Volunteer Infantry Regiment, known as the Orange Blossom Boys. The 124th New York was to hold the extreme left flank of the Union defenses on Houck's Ridge. Coming at them were the 4th and 5th Texas brigades of Confederate Gen. John Bell Hood's division with three regiments of Gen. Henry L. Benning's Georgia Brigade in support directly behind them. To make things worse for the Orange Blossom Boys, these particular Confederate soldiers had marched all day and were itching for a fight.

The fighting between the 124th New York and the Texans went back and forth over the top wall three times. The first charge of the New Yorkers ended with the death of their beloved commander, Col. Augustus Van Horne Ellis, who was shot in the forehead and fell dead off his horse. Ironically, on the march to Gettysburg, Ellis prophesied that he would not survive the battle. Maj. James Cromwell rallied the men of the 124th and bravely rode through a storm of bullets in order to retrieve the body of his colonel. According to eyewitness testimony, Cromwell was so gallant that some of the Texans shouted, "Don't shoot at him … don't kill him," but to no avail. He and his gray horse were both shot and killed at the bottom of the field.

The New Yorkers charged a third and final time to retrieve both of their officers' bodies, which they did. However, the Texans gained the wall, and as the Georgians moved up beside them, the Texans jumped up and fired a volley at Smith's Battery, causing horses and men to tumble to the ground. As the Georgians jumped over the wall, Smith was able to save only one of his artillery guns from being captured by the enemy. Eventually, the 124th New York was overrun by fresh Confederate troops, who secured Devil's Den and the southern part of Houck's Ridge. These assaults by Hood's brigades left hundreds of men on both sides killed and more than 1,500 seriously wounded.

Over the years, I've interviewed many eyewitnesses while investigating this area of the battlefield. Once, while filming near

Smith's Battery, two woman shared a fascinating story with me. Apparently, their husbands were Union reenactors, and they had come to Gettysburg as part of a living history event during the anniversary of the battle. One evening, the two men (dressed in full reenactment gear) were having a casual conversation while leaning on one of the boulders between Smith's Battery and the 124th New York monuments. As they discussed the day's events, they heard a group of people walking off to their right. When they turned to look, four Union soldiers came into view, their muskets casually slung over their shoulders. They looked tired, drawn and dusty, and they crossed the road towards the wall at the top of the Triangular Field, which is adjacent to Devil's Den. One of the soldiers looked over, gave them an approving nod with his head, and continued on.

This Confederate sharpshooter met his violent end at Devil's Den.

One of the husbands commented that something about those men was odd. He couldn't explain why, but he thought they were out of place. The four soldiers certainly looked the part, but it seemed almost too real. He tapped his buddy and said, "Let's go talk to those guys, they really fit the part."

Only a few seconds had passed since they saw the four "reenactors," allowing them plenty of time to catch up to them, but when they reached the wall of the Triangular Field, they couldn't find the uniformed men anywhere. In fact, only one other person was there — a man standing at the wall looking into the field. They asked him if he had seen any other reenactors walk by. He replied that he had been standing there for about 10 minutes and they were the first people he had seen since he arrived.

They searched the area in vain and left scratching their heads. What had they just witnessed? The four soldiers looked as solid as the rocks they were leaning on. The eerily authentic condition of their uniforms was certainly impressive, but they were almost too authentic. The tired looks, the dust-covered uniforms, the drawn, almost-sad faces. Did they witness a scene from the past — four Union soldiers walking across Houck's Ridge after the battle had ended? Or maybe it was before the second day's brutality began?

And what about the brief interaction that occurred? The four soldiers knew the two reenactors were there, and one of them apparently acknowledged that with a nod. Could it have been a rip in the fabric of time, a rare moment when the veil between past, present and future is lifted, leaving those who witness the anomaly with a very strange experience to recount to others? Or were they four spirits, bonded in death as they were in life, casualties of one of history's most violent clashes?

Strangely enough, profound stories like this one abound within the reenactor community. Maybe the ghost soldiers see men dressed like them and are drawn to the familiar surroundings they knew while alive. Most reenactors feel a strong connection to the battles and soldiers they honor. Many are descendants whose great-great-great-grandfathers or uncles died in these battles. Others retain vivid and accurate memories as if they were actually participants in these battles, which suggest evidence of possible reincarnation. Whatever the case, reenactors represent ideal witnesses to all types of paranormal activity associated with historic events. In the case of Gettysburg, they are inexplicably drawn to the energy, and many times they offer unique insight regarding the mysterious nature of this most hallowed ground.

CLIMBING THE WALLS

At the western end of Devil's Den lies the Triangular Field, into which the phantom soldiers described above seem to have disappeared. The stone wall at the top of this down-sloping field has changed little since local farmers built them in the days before the Civil War. When clearing this Pennsylvania field for crops, they hauled the stones to the side, forming the walls that soldiers later used for protection during the fierce fighting that took place there. In retrospect, it did little to lessen the carnage.

On the first day of the battle of Gettysburg, the Confederates routed Union troops and drove them back through town, but the Federals managed to keep hold of the high ground to the south and east. When the sun rose on the morning of July 2, both were entrenched, but the Army of the Potomac had formed its troops in a hook-like formation that ran from Culp's Hill and Spangler's Spring all the way to Little Round Top. Emboldened by his army's success the previous day, Confederate Gen. Robert E. Lee attached little importance to this topographical disadvantage and launched the Army of Northern Virginia in multiple attacks against the Union flanks

After a lengthy delay to assemble his forces and avoid detection in his approach march, Lt. Gen. James Longstreet attacked with his First Corps against the Union left flank. As part of this en echelon (diagonal) style of attack, a division under the command of Maj. Gen. John Bell Hood was ordered to assault Devil's Den and Little Round Top. In order to accomplish this, Gen. Hood had to first maneuver several of his regiments through the Rose Woods and up the slope of the Triangular Field.

A seasoned soldier who understood that achieving his objective would play a key role in Gen. Lee's efforts to dislodge Union forces, Hood selected some of his best fighting men to lead the attack. At approximately 4:30 p.m., the 3rd Arkansas and the 1st, 4th, and 5th Texas, as well as the 2nd, 15th, 17th and 20th Georgia, began their advance. When lead elements of the 1st Texas reached the stone wall, a deadly onslaught of Union artillery and rifle fire awaited. The effect was devastating. Men screamed as each side fired their muskets at point blank range. As thick smoke filled the air, their breathing and vision became limited. Those who had bayonets fixed stabbed at fleeting shadows; others used their rifles as clubs. Smoke lay on the field like a blanket, but small eddies of air cleared the way for a brief view of the violence that had taken place just moments before.

A soldier who was there recalled the fighting:

Reenactors often have close encounters with ghost soldiers at Gettysburg.

"Roaring cannon, crashing rifles, screeching shots, bursting shells, hissing bullets, cheers, shouts, shrieks and groans were the notes of the song of death which greeted the grim reaper, as with mighty sweeps he leveled down the richest field of grain ever garnered on this continent."

As one can only imagine, the Triangular Field is replete with encounters of ghost soldiers still fighting the good fight. Many battlefield visitors have experienced camera malfunctions while trying to take pictures of it. A few years ago, one man took some video footage near a grouping of rocks in the middle of the field. He said he was drawn to the spot and felt overwhelmed with sadness once he got there. When he returned home, he played the videotape and heard a loud, prolonged moan as if a man was writhing in agony. Impossible, he thought, remembering that he was alone in the field when he shot the video.

People have reported seeing Confederate sharpshooters crouched behind the rocks at the bottom of the field. To their utter dismay, some visitors have actually seen impressions in the grass actually moving towards them, and Union soldiers have been sighted and photographed at the gate entrance. Others have heard spectral sounds, including cannon fire, gun shots, screams, moans and the galloping of horses.

In the fall of 2001, video cameras with infrared capability had just become available, and only a handful of paranormal investigators were using camcorder systems to capture images in the dark. After doing some research on Gettysburg, I decided that the Triangular Field would be an ideal place to shoot some infrared video. On this particular visit, two friends accompanied my family and me to the battlefield for a weekend campout. Both Dennis and Charles had served in the military, and I told them about my theory on capturing historical moments on film. After a nice campfire meal, we left our families and ventured out onto the battlefield.

We started at the Devil's Den parking lot and climbed up through the boulders to the top of Houck's Ridge. I stopped at the Union battery monument, and I could almost feel the sense of apprehension that these artillerymen must have felt as they saw their infantry comrades dying on the field below. As I walked towards the upper wall of the Triangular Field, I turned on my Sony Night-Shot camcorder and began to film. I asked permission of any spirits present to capture their images on my camcorder — or to at least record what the battle sounded like. When I got to the wall, Dennis proceeded to climb over and lean on it. Charles stood just behind my left shoulder as I called out for the boys to come forth and join us.

Within seconds a series of energy signatures sped across my LED screen. I told Dennis and Charles to head into the field while I filmed from behind the wall. As Charles moved over the wall, I saw a man dressed in a white shirt and black pants walking about halfway up the slope of the field towards the wall. At this point, my senses were at full alert, as the energy in the field was intense and I knew something was going to happen.

These two video captures show the formation of an apparition near the stone wall at the top of The Triangular Field.

As I filmed the man walking, I saw a movement behind him and suddenly felt a rush of wind go by me. I refocused on the area to his left where Dennis and Charles had gone to sit down. Feeling drawn to that side of the field, I looked to my right and filmed along the wall. I swept the field briefly with the camera but had an overwhelming urge to film to my right again. I turned and saw the man from earlier getting closer to the wall, so I steadied the camera on him. As I focused, I heard a little voice in my head say, "Hold steady. You're not going to want to miss this!" So I fixed the camcorder on him until the feeling dissipated about a minute later.

This capture shows a ghost soldier crossing over a stone wall in The Triangular Field in front of a living person.

While reviewing the footage later that night, we knew immediately that we had captured something extremely rare: a full-bodied, detailed apparition moving on video. In the playback, as the real man walks towards the wall, another individual — semi-transparent and in Civil War uniform — manifests in front of him, running frantically towards the wall. Without slowing down, he jerks his leg up and over as if trying to jump it ... an astounding visual to say the least. Stunned, Dennis and Charles asked me what in the world I had just taped. Trying to be as logical and objective as possible, I concluded that we may have just documented one of two things: 1) a residual haunting in which we captured the playback of a soldier actually running towards the wall during the battle; or 2) the spirit of a soldier who honored my request to show us what the battle must have been like that day.

In either case, this video footage remains one of the most profound and compelling pieces of evidence we've ever captured. The implications are staggering. When analyzed objectively, it leaves little wiggle room for debunkers. There, in plain view for everyone to see, is a full-bodied apparition whose appearance and actions tie in directly to the location in which the video was shot — a Civil War soldier running for his life. The only thing the video doesn't convey is the horror that this poor young man must have been feeling at the time.

But how could my video camera capture something I didn't see while shooting it? Many contemporary paranormal researchers believe that ghosts exist as some form of electromagnetic energy, and science dictates that all energy is traceable in the light spectrum. When I first decided to investigate battlefields, I wanted to prove beyond a shadow of a doubt that lost souls still roamed the places where they died tragically. I could attempt to capture ghostly images by using an ultraviolet filter on my 35mm camera, but then I would only be capturing a still image. Ideally, I wanted to capture an apparition in movement, and to do that I needed a camcorder. I tested a variety of models that claimed to have infrared — or nighttime — capability. After several months of experimenting, I chose the Sony "Night-shot" system, which allows the shooter to film up to 10 feet away in complete darkness.

Although there's no official manual that describes how to use a camcorder to capture ghosts, I believe that you can increase your chances of success. As a sensitive, I use my intuition when attempting to record the past and listen to that little voice inside my head that always leads me down the right path. We all have it; some of us just listen more intently to it than others. By quieting the mind, I've learned how to gather information from both residual imprints and direct telepathic communication with discarnate spirits. This method can be applied to obtaining video evidence by allowing yourself to be immersed in the energies that surround you — or, as some would say, tuning into the frequencies associated with paranormal activity.

I've found that the best way to connect to other realms is to slowly ramp up your skill through measured exercises. As the old adage goes, practice makes perfect! For example, find a comfortable chair that allows you to sit with your back straight and your feet firmly on the floor. Close your eyes and take a deep breath through your nose for a long count of four, expanding your diaphragm to the maximum. Next, breathe out to a count of three. Repeat this three or four times as you attempt to clear your head of all thoughts and quiet the noise in your mind. Once you've achieved this, count to 10. Remember, the only thing that you should be focused on is the current number, nothing else. For example, if you think to yourself as you're focusing on the number three, "Wow, this is easy," or "What should I make for dinner tonight," you failed to be fully focused and need to start over again.

How can this simple exercise help you to capture paranormal evidence on a battlefield? Communicating with the spirits of those who have passed on requires an enormous amount of focus, and these mental exercises will help you with that. If you can tune into the energies around you, you'll be able to locate those areas that are more likely to "host" a paranormal event. Therefore, you'll have a better chance of capturing historical moments with whatever equipment you might be using. Clearing the mind is the first step to being able to feel the spirit energies around us. And remember, always ask permission to interact with them (or capture their image or voice) so that you can share their stories with others and keep their memories alive.

— Patrick Burke

CHAPTER 4 - FIRST SIGHTING

"It is only those who have neither fired a shot nor heard the shrieks and groans of the wounded who cry aloud for blood, more vengeance, more desolation. War is hell."

- General William Tecumseh Sherman

On May 8, 2004, I experienced what I believe to have been my first apparitional sighting as a field investigator. It occurred at a prominent location on the Gettysburg battlefield known as Spangler's Spring, where Union troops of the 12th Corps constructed earthworks and heavy fighting took place as both armies attempted to occupy Culp's Hill. After the war, many veterans conveyed how temporary truces were called between the sides so that men from both armies could fill their canteens with water from the spring. This particular part of the battlefield has become popular as a result of both these anecdotal soldier's stories and ongoing reports of paranormal activity.

Our investigative team recorded the following testimony immediately after our strange encounter. Four individuals, including myself, who were either witness to the apparition itself or some other related phenomena share their stories here. Others present at the time of the encounter are also mentioned throughout our conversation.

Jack: I definitely saw something moving by the tree line at the edge of the woods. It was a glowing white object. At first, I thought it was a rock. You know how some of the rocks have a lot of white moss or bacteria covering them, so at first I thought it was a rock, but then it started moving. It was almost like it moved out from behind one of the rocks and moved back in.

Sara: Exactly! Went back in! Donna was over there and she had the same experience, and as we were all moving forward toward the object, she was moving sideways with the object. And so there was clearly, clearly something at the tree line.

Many people have reported seeing flashes of light at Spangler's Spring.

Jack: Yeah, and then again it was hard because it was the gloaming time of day ... dusk ... and you know your eyes can play tricks on you with that type of light. But I really did see a glowing figure moving back and forth. And then five minutes later I saw something move again, and I went running over there because I wanted to make sure there wasn't a guy in a bright white shirt walking by or a white-tailed deer hopping along the tree line, but there was nothing like that there, so it was definitely odd.

Milo: I was on top of the hill. My K-11 EMF meter was going crazy. I was getting lots of spikes. It was funny because I thought Scott was with me. At the beginning, we were walking up the hill and I thought Scott was still next to me while we were up there. I thought he was over in the woods filming me, but I realized "No, there's nobody over there." But my meter was spiking and I felt there was somebody behind me; I got a pretty good-sized orb picture.

Jon: The area was in between Spangler's Spring and the trail leading up to Culp's Hill, and Eric had walked that way as well. He said he kept feeling like there was someone behind him, and he kept looking behind his shoulder ... and he kept looking like there was something up there. I felt the exact same thing. I had walked up and basically everyone else was at the bottom of the hill. I wasn't planning on going up to the top of the hill; I was planning on going about four or five turns and just standing up there because a lot of times things happen to me when there's nobody else anywhere around to verify it. So it's just my word against everyone else's. So I went up there and kept looking around. I had this feeling like I had to keep looking out, and keep on looking out because I had to make sure that you know ... they weren't behind me. Eric went up just a few minutes later, and he got the same feeling.

Close up of glowing anomaly.

Milo: Right. I walked up the trail because Jon had just come down from there and he said that he felt like there was something up there. So I went up with my meter to see if there was something going on.

Jon: And the interesting thing is I never told him. I said, "You may want to check out further up the hill; there seems to be an electric charge or something up there." I actually told some other people the exact same thing because I really felt like something was going to happen. I never told Milo how I felt, and then one of the first things he said when he came down was, "I kind of feel like there's somebody back there." It's just one of those strange things. When we first got to Gettysburg we were exhausted, but none of us had ever been here before and Jack mentioned how he felt extremely emotional for no particular reason. Melissa felt sad, and I felt like there was a drumming of energy across the entire battlefield. I've been to many active haunted houses, but this is the first time I've ever felt like an entire town and battlefield feel like one huge haunted house. It feels like there's always something going on right beneath the surface or just past the range of our senses. It's just strange ... very strange to actually be walking through a large environment like that, and just not being able to feel alone at any point.

Jack: I agree completely. This place is amazing. We may not be able to prove there was an apparition near those woods tonight, but we can certainly corroborate some pretty compelling evidence that suggests "something" paranormal did occur. We should go back there later tonight or tomorrow morning and set up some infrared cameras.

In order to fully appreciate this account, one must first understand the spontaneous nature of apparitions. The late Andrew McKenzie, a paranormal researcher for the Society for Psychical Research (SPR), said that although members of the general public regard apparitions (or ghosts) as the spirits of the dead returning to manifest themselves to the living, it is far too simple a view of the phenomena. F.W.H. Myers, a founder of the SPR, agreed, saying that "Whatever else, indeed, a 'ghost' may be, it is probably one of the most complex phenomena in nature."

Reenactors at Spangler's Spring

With this in mind, one must allow for the possibility that some sort of shift in consciousness occurs when experiencing a "visual" manifestation of a ghost. During most apparitional experiences, for example, the act of looking away from the apparition, even for a moment, causes the figure to disappear. McKenzie reasoned that the act of looking away might trigger a change of consciousness. In fact, most researchers generally accept that people experience apparitions in what are termed "altered states of consciousness."

Andrew Nichols, noted parapsychologist and founder of the American Institute of Parapsychology, stresses that most apparitional encounters fall into the category of "crisis apparitions," a phenomena during which people see the apparitions of friends or relatives appear before them at the very moment of the loved one's death. Such apparitions, he adds, are isolated psychic events and are usually never seen again, but if the apparition appears again and again over a long period of time, then the house (or battlefield) is considered genuinely haunted.

Regarding our experience at Spangler's Spring, we might lean toward the explanation of a genuine haunting as opposed to a crisis apparition, especially considering the location and its history. This represents a particularly compelling encounter because multiple witnesses saw the same apparition, which is very rare. Other corroborative evidence also exists, as Jon and Milo felt an electrically charged atmosphere on the path just above where and at approximately the same time the apparition was seen. Milo also recorded electromagnetic spikes on his EMF meter, which validates that some type of atmospheric anomaly was taking place during the same time period.

Personally, it was a watershed moment. I never believed I would ever actually see an apparition, as years of field research had yielded many profound experiences but never an actual ghost sighting. Did we witness the genuine haunting of a restless soldier's spirit still wandering the grounds on which he experienced a violent, sudden and premature death? Or was it a replay of a battlefield moment forever etched into the environment — perhaps of a soldier cautiously emerging from the tree line in order to quench his thirst?

Either way, it seems fitting the experience occurred at Gettysburg, a place where, as Jon acutely noted, " … it feels like there's always something going on right beneath the surface or just past the range of our senses."

— Jack Roth

CHAPTER 5 – THE GIFT

"Never in the field of human conflict was so much owed by so many to so few."

- Sir Winston Churchill

The old wooden gate at the top of The Triangular Field.

It was a cool and pleasant August evening in 2007 when Darryl "Smitty" Smith, Michael Hartness and I decided to visit our old ghost soldier buddies at the Triangular Field. Mike, unlike many of us on the American Battlefield Ghost Hunter's Society (ABGHS) team, had never experienced anything out of the ordinary at this location, but his luck was about to change (for better or worse).

Mike desperately wanted to have a first-hand paranormal encounter, and knowing what kind of compelling evidence the team had captured in the Triangular Field on past visits made him even more anxious to experience something. The Triangular Field offers as good an opportunity to have a paranormal encounter as any other place in Gettysburg, as unsuspecting visitors to this field have reported many strange accounts over the years. This makes perfect sense, as some of the most vicious fighting of the Civil War took place in this small field between Devil's Den and the Wheatfield during the second day of the battle.

As we approached the stone wall at the top of the field, I decided to stir up whatever paranormal energies I could. "Hey, boys!" I yelled out into the field. "We're back and it sure would be great if ya'll would honor us with a bit of what happened here on July 2, 1863. I know Mike would surely appreciate it."

A great deal of energy from the battle seems to have been absorbed at The Triangular Field.

Smitty moved over to the gate at the upper wall and proceeded to film the area where I captured an apparition crossing the wall in 2001 (see Chapter 3: There's the Devil to Pay). Mike and I walked down to the middle of the field, near the right side of the wall as you walk down toward the bottom. The Triangular Field is normally quite active with visitors and ghost hunters, but on this particular day very few people were present. I walked down the sloped field approximately 20 paces apart from Mike and turned my camcorder toward the undergrowth, some of which stood more than six feet tall. Due to the height of the grass, I couldn't see into the wooded area where the 3rd Arkansas and 1st Texas charged Houck's Ridge during the battle.

Suddenly there was a rush of air, and we heard what sounded like hundreds of people moving in the woods. We both looked at each other at the same time and asked simultaneously, "Do you hear that!"

The noise got louder as this "attacking force" appeared to get closer to us. The air around us suddenly pulsated as if it had taken on a life of its own. I knew immediately that Mike and I had stepped fully into a paranormal moment, one of those rare moments when the very fabric of time "rips open" and reveals — albeit briefly — what happened long ago. Every one of our senses was heightened, and we could actually distinguish all the sounds associated with a mass of moving soldiers — rifle butts smacking low branches, canteens slapping hips, and the tramp of thousands of feet on dry leaves and twigs. I ran up the hill as Mike came towards me. We found a break in the grass, and as we turned down this path we were surrounded by the sound of men running. I could hear the sounds of labored breathing and muttering voices when a sudden flash in my mind's eye showed a glimpse of the men before me. With our hearts beating faster than you could ever imagine, we ran towards the wall. I held the camcorder over my head, pointing it towards the woods in the hopes of catching something through the grass. When I reached the wall I brought the camera back down. Finally, I thought to myself, I might be able to capture the actual historical battle on film. I seriously believed that elusive moment might actually be at hand. Then, a woman with a small group of people behind us shouted, "Hey! You find anything!"

At that moment the paranormal event stopped, and the regular night noises returned to the environment. Mike and I looked at each other and laughed; we realized we had just been graced with the ability to view living history from those who actually participated in it — getting a glimpse of actual historic events as they occurred almost a century and a half earlier. At times like this one is often speechless. We smiled at the woman and answered, "Nah, nothing here."

We asked for a personal experience, and we truly believe our buddies on the other side heard us and gave us an astounding gift. Whenever I have an experience like this on a battlefield, I feel extremely humbled. The fact that these brave souls feel connected enough with me to actually allow me to witness history as it really happened is just incredible, and I'm truly grateful for it.

— Patrick Burke

CHAPTER 6 ~ RECORDINGS FROM ANOTHER REALM

"I hate war as only a soldier who has lived it can, only as one who has seen its brutality, its futility, its stupidity."

- President Dwight D. Eisenhower

Electronic Voice Phenomena, or EVP, represents one of the most fascinating mysteries associated with ghosts and hauntings. Basically, EVP is the reception of voice or other sound on an audiotape for which there is no known environmental source. The phenomenon is the subject of great debate within the paranormal community. Those who view the phenomenon as truly paranormal believe the recordings are either the voices of the dead trying to communicate or other residual sounds emanating from the paranormal realm. In Gettysburg, these might include cannon fire, gunshots, screams, and other sounds associated with the 1863 battle that have somehow been imprinted onto the environment and subsequently picked up on an audio recording. Skeptics, on the other hand, believe EVP recordings are nothing more than natural sounds falsely interpreted as paranormal in nature.

My experience with EVP tells me that both camps are correct, depending on the actual recording in question. On the one hand, many recordings capture compelling evidence of either attempted communication from the dead or residual sounds from past events. On the other hand, the human mind is the greatest puzzle solver in the known universe. Scott Flagg, chief operating officer for the American Institute of Parapsychology and paranormal researcher, suggests that each of us must recognize our own mind's ability and desire to piece information together. As a result, simple background garble can be interpreted as actual words or specific sounds by the brain, and many recordings can be misinterpreted as paranormal in nature when in fact they aren't.

"I've personally stood around a circle of eight people listening very intently to a possible EVP recording and heard no less than eight different interpretations of what the purported voice was saying," says Flagg. His advice: Avoid manipulating audio except for removing background noise, adjusting volume and isolating elements. This will minimize the mind's opportunity to create something from nothing.

Theories abound as to how EVP might work. The Low Frequency Theory suggests that EVP occurs below the normal range of hearing (pressure waves from 0Hz to 20Hz), and that somehow audio devices are able to record in this range. The EMF Theory proposes that ghosts organize random electromagnetic fields to create EVP. If so, a TV set between channels or a radio tuned between stations can provide the static with which it is thought ghosts manipulate in order to "speak." A new theory suggests that very low frequency electromagnetic fields (0Hz to 30Hz) can stimulate a variety of small objects, including air molecules, into motion. This process creates pressure waves that can be heard by our ears.

Regardless of how it might work, people have been interested in its applications since electronic recording devices were first invented. As early as 1928, Thomas Edison started working on equipment he hoped would permit communication with the dead. Nobody seems to know for sure how far he got with his experiments because he died before he published any results. Over time, research organizations such as the Research Association for Voice Taping and the American Association of Electronic Voice Phenomena were founded to further our understanding of this complex enigma. One of the great pioneers of EVP research was Sarah Estep, who recorded more than 20,000 voices that she claimed were other-dimensional, extra-terrestrial, or from loved ones who had passed on. She developed a classification system for EVP recordings, which is as follows:

Class A: A clear and distinct voice that can be heard without the use of headphones and can be duplicated onto other tapes.

Class B: A voice that is sometimes distinct, fairly loud and can sometimes be heard without the use of headphones.

Class C: A faint and whispery voice that can barely be heard and is sometimes indecipherable.

Although the focus of EVP tends to be on voice communication, we should never overlook the importance of residual or imprinted sounds that often are captured on recording devices. This especially applies to a place like Gettysburg, where specific sounds are intricately connected to the environment's emotional blueprint. In fact, the frequency of EVP in the form of gunshots, cannon fire, hooves clopping and metal clanging (military accoutrements) recorded at Gettysburg is much greater than that of communicative voices. This also applies to music, as some of the most compelling EVP I've ever heard are the sounds of music forever imprinted during the battle — "Dixie," fife and drum music, and other period melodies.

The Baladerry Inn once served as a field hospital during the battle.

Over the years, we've collected extremely compelling EVP during our investigations at Gettysburg. In addition to the EVP mentioned above, we documented several other accounts from the battlefield. The first is from a field investigator named Coby, who was boarding with the rest of our investigative team at the Baladerry Inn Bed & Breakfast when he recorded an EVP. The Baladerry Inn is located on the actual battlefield and was used as a field hospital during and after the battle. Bloodstains can still be seen on parts of the wooden floors. The building is also very active from a paranormal standpoint.

Here is Coby's account, which was verified by team members after analysis:

In the early morning hours (approximately 4 a.m.) of May 7, 2004, two voices (a and b) were recorded from our room at the Baladerry Inn when we kept getting woken up for no apparent reason. Ellie took photos of the room when my K-11 EMF meter started going crazy. At this time we were simply sitting up in bed talking. There are small orbs in the picture (confirmed). The voice recorder was located by the closet in the corner of the room.

a) Ellie (to Coby): We have to get that before we go ...

Voice (female – very matter-of-factly): How?

... and then seconds later ...

b) Voice (male – sighing or whispering): Okay

After analyzing the recording thoroughly, we classified this as a Class A EVP, as both voices were very clear and easy to make out. They also seemed genuine as opposed to residual, meaning some sort of communication was going on between the discarnate voices and the people staying in the room. This cannot be verified of course, but it constitutes very compelling EVP evidence.

The second account occurred during the same weekend investigation. While investigating at Spangler's Spring on the evening of May 7, 2004, we coordinated various team members to establish secluded areas in which to conduct EVP experiments. We asked a particular field investigator named Heather to take her micro-cassette recorder and sit on a rock by the actual spring. Once there, she performed an EVP experiment during which she asked certain questions in 20-second intervals, thus providing enough time for a possible response. Upon playback of

Bloody floorboards.

her tape, she ran to us in a rather excited state and suggested she may have captured something. When we listened to the recording, we all heard the following very clearly at the midpoint of her questioning:

Heather: Do you like it here?

Voice (male — low but clearly audible): Hell no!

Once again, we classified this as a Class A EVP. The voice was male, and you could hear the words "Hell no!" very distinctly on the tape. It was most likely a genuine contact, as a form of conscious energy was clearly responding to her question. Unfortunately, in regards to Heather's recording, the voice she captured mysteriously disappeared after a couple of weeks. At first we thought she must have accidentally erased it, but she was adamant about being careful with it. Plus, EVP mysteriously disappearing from magnetic tape is not unheard of. There are many instances when EVP has been captured and then "uncaptured," as if the sound was only audible for a short period of time.

EVP is a promising, yet frustrating, area of study within the world of paranormal research. There are only so many ways one can analyze EVP recordings. You can utilize sound programs to clean them up (eliminate background noise, etc.), and you can use computer programs to analyze sound waves and determine at what frequency these sounds are emanating. But as of now we have no way to determine if these recordings are from another realm or simply the result of our minds making sense of chaos.

– Jack Roth

CHAPTER 7 ~ MANIACAL MAELSTROM OF SOUND

"Humanize war?
You might as well talk about humanizing hell!"

- British Admiral Jacky Fisher

The Cemetery Gatehouse on Cemetery Hill.

Confederate Maj. Gen. Richard Ewell

As I stood on the edge of the Brickyard Road, my right foot resting near the 7th West Virginia left flank marker, I let my mind travel back in time. The summer heat I was experiencing was nothing like the heat on July 2, 1863, which was, reportedly, downright oppressive. I looked over the fields where the Confederate troops of Maj. Gen. Richard Ewell's Second Corp traversed in order to get to the bottom of the steep incline on the east side of Cemetery Hill, and I wondered how any of those brave souls could actually have made it through the cannonade and musketry fire.

The 11th and 12th Corps of the Army of the Potomac sat waiting, entrenched in front of a mass of cannons that bristled out in every direction, like a porcupine's quills, defending all the approaches the Confederates might use to attack the far right flank of the Union line. I imagined the skirmish line — comprised of the 41st New York and 33rd Massachusetts — and saw them standing (or in most cases lying down or kneeling on one knee), watching a massive gray line come towards them. I saw a fleeting shadow out in the middle of the field where the Union skirmishers would have been waiting in front of the steep incline to the top of Cemetery Hill. I felt a chill, the kind that only happens when spirit energy is around me. The energy reminded me of a firsthand account from a Union soldier from the 41st New York. He reported that suddenly, through the smoke, the Rebels were on them. He fired one shot and chaos ensued around him.

"We held the line for about one minute, and then we broke and

ran back to the safety of our lines."

Confederate Col. Isaac Avery of the 6th North Carolina led his brigade forward as part of the initial advance that day, with Gen. Harry T. Hays' Louisiana Tigers surging on his right. By the time Avery and his troops reached the cover of the bottom of the hill, however, they were already winded. They needed to catch their breath before pushing on to the heights. Huddled at the bottom of the hill, they were perfect targets for Union Col. Leopold Von Gilsa's 41st New York Infantry, who hid behind makeshift breastworks and rifle pits and fired down into the Confederate ranks.

With sheer determination and in perfect sync, Hays and Avery's brigades charged up the steep slope with bayonets fixed, gave a rebel yell and smashed into the Union defenders. They overran Von Gilsa's infantry and engaged the cannoneers, who were busy loading and firing cannons. Fierce hand-to-hand combat ensued, with the cannoneers using ramrods and whatever pieces of equipment they could find as weapons. Avery and Hays pressed forward, forcing the federals from their guns and taking charge of a key strategic position.
I could only imagine what it must have been like for the Union soldiers defending that hill:

Your cannons open up a brisk and affective fire, you think that should do them, but then you see the line, through brief gaps of the smoke-filled field, closing rank and steadily advancing. Before you know it an order is given to ready arms and fire. Hot lead is zipping around you, men are falling to the left and right of you, and then that god-awful scream from thousands of throats ... the rebel yell washes over you and the Confederates smash into your line. It holds for a minute, and then you are racing back to the safety of your entrenched comrades on the slope of Cemetery Hill.

As a result of heroic fighting by the rebels, the welfare of the entire Army of the Potomac lay in the balance. Confederate Maj. Samuel Tate of the 6th North Carolina later described the action:

"Seventy-five North Carolinians of the Sixth Regiment and 12

Louisianans of Hays' brigade scaled the walls and planted the colors of the 6th North Carolina and 9th Louisiana on the guns. It was fully dark. The enemy stood with tenacity never before displayed by them, but with bayonet, clubbed musket, sword, pistols and rocks from the wall, we cleared the heights and silenced the guns."

But with no support forthcoming, the brave Confederate assault was doomed. While leading his troops forward, Avery fell from his horse bleeding, shot through the neck. Understanding the mortality of his wound, he scribbled a note that he handed to a subordinate. The note simply read, "Tell my father I died with my face to the enemy." Avery died of his wounds the following day. Eventually, the Confederates had to retreat as a result of overwhelming pressure from Union reinforcements. The second day's fighting ended — after much carnage and death — with little ground gained or lost by either side.

Another interesting aspect of the East Cemetery Hill fighting was that it could have been avoided altogether if not for a fateful decision made the day before. On the first day of fighting, the Rebels had pushed the Yankees all the way through Gettysburg to the slight heights overlooking the town. If Confederate Gen. John B. Gordon would have roused his brigade, day two may have looked a lot different, if in fact fighting was necessary at all. Gen. Richard S. Ewell, Gordon's commander, had instructed him to "take that wooded hill to the west of Cemetery Hill and occupy it." Gordon informed Ewell that his brigade had taken the brunt of the attack and were, in his exact words, "done in." This 30-second exchange may very well have changed the outcome of the battle, and in turn American history. But history doesn't favor hindsight. On that day and forever more, a particular outcome was firmly etched into the fabric of time.

As paranormal investigators, our goal on Cemetery Hill — 145 years later — was to attempt to capture some semblance of the fabled rebel yell. Having sent chills down the spines of many Union soldiers, this unnerving sound has been described in various ways, but the general consensus was that if you heard that yell, you knew that hell on earth was coming. Confederate Col. Keller Anderson of Kentucky's Orphan Brigade described it best when he said:

"Then arose that do-or-die expression, that maniacal maelstrom of sound; that penetrating, rasping, shrieking, blood-curdling noise that could be heard for miles and whose volume reached the heavens — such an expression as never yet came from the throats of sane men, but from men whom the seething blast of an imaginary hell would not check while the sound lasted."

With my brother John and friend Mike Hartness accompanying me, we headed to the base of East Cemetery Hill where Avery led the North Carolinians. I turned on my audio recorder and asked the question I had asked 100 times before: "Would you brave men allow me to capture just a bit of what happened here on July 2, 1863 ... whether it be the rebel yell or the Union huzza, or any other sounds of combat. I would be honored if you gave me a picture or the rebel yell."

There are times when a paranormal investigator gets what might be considered a special piece of evidence that is more of a personal gift than a random capture. It's a unique moment, when time seems to shift back and allows you to see or hear what happened on that spot years ago. On this day, the brave men who gave their lives for their cause were listening to my request, and, somehow, they made it happen.

When I played back the EVP I first heard what sounded like a gunshot, and then another, and then a very distinct yell. Shocked that I may have captured the actual rebel yell as an EVP, I compared my audio to a rare recording of the rebel yell at a 1913 reunion of the veterans of the Battle of Gettysburg. In the documentary footage, Confederate veterans are at the bloody angle wall — where Confederate Gen. Lewis A. Armistead's brigade temporarily breeched the Union line during Pickett's Charge — facing the Union veterans who defended the wall 50 years earlier. Suddenly, you hear one of the Confederate veterans give the rebel yell as he twirled his hat over his head. A Union veteran responds, as if startled, "There it is, that's the rebel yell."

When we compared the EVP to the audio of the old Southern veteran, we noticed that, although the veteran's voice was much older, the cadence and style were almost exactly the same. Was this a residual playback manifested by my thoughts and energy intermingling with the imprinted energies from the battle? Possibly. Or, just maybe it was a ghost soldier who understood that a kindred spirit yearned to hear what had not been heard for a very, very long time.

— Patrick Burke

CHAPTER 8 – GETTYSBURG'S QUANTUM QUIRKS

"The most beautiful thing we can experience is the mysterious. It is the source of all true art and science. He to whom this emotion is a stranger, who can no longer pause to wonder and stand rapt in awe, is as good as dead; his eyes are closed."

- Albert Einstein

Dead Confederate Soldiers at the edge of Rose Woods.

For some, experiencing Gettysburg can be likened to peering down the proverbial rabbit hole. Energy vortices captured on film and video, strange wavy-like ripples in the atmosphere seen with the naked eye, high electro- and geomagnetic readings garnered from high-tech equipment, and other strange anomalies experienced on almost every portion of the battlefield. But what do these highly unfamiliar events represent?

Extensive volumes have been written regarding the relationship between paranormal phenomena and the non-traditional scientific possibilities that might validate them as part of the natural and known universe. Quantum physics explores the realities of life at the sub-atomic levels, and this has had consequences in terms of our own consciousness and experience, as well as our relationship to the universe around us. Quantum theory suggests there are interconnections and influences between subject and object, which, according to traditional scientific theory, cannot exist. This opens the door to alternative explanations of consciousness and challenges us to explore them with an open-mindedness that goes against a societal belief system still entrenched in superstition, fear and skepticism.

As it relates to Gettysburg, how might quantum physics explain the paranormal phenomena encountered there on a regular basis? How can a man see the "imprint" of a Union regiment marching near the Wheatfield more than a century earlier? How can a video camera capture a ghost soldier jumping over a fence at the Triangular Field? How can we hear the sounds of battles already fought? Can we experience history first-hand, as a result of some universal law of physics scientists haven't discovered yet?

For more than a century, the greatest minds on this planet have studied paranormal phenomena and their implications on our understanding of the universe and human consciousness. Theories associated with time slips or time warps can be traced to Albert Einstein, who proposed the theory that time and space form a continuum that bends, folds or warps from the observer's point of view, relative to such factors as movement or gravitation. A time slip, therefore, might be a perceived discontinuity in time, either one that allows something to travel backward or forward in time, or an area of space that appears to travel through time at a different rate from the rest of the universe. If we assume these discontinuities are possible, it might explain how a couple who visited the Gettysburg battlefield in 1989 reportedly had a conversation with a barefoot, emaciated, sweat-soaked man dressed in a filthy, ripped, gray uniform who politely

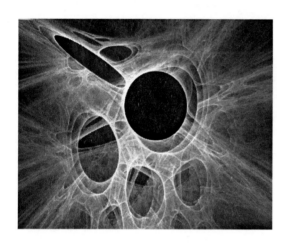

asked for a drink of water, then slowly disappeared before their eyes!

Mathematical developments associated with the superstring theory, considered by some scientists to be the most outrageous theory ever proposed, may help theoretical physicists explain encounters with the past as well. Research suggests that disruptions and warps can occur naturally in space, resulting infrequently in theoretically possible random time events. These warps or disruptions might allow for any action or event to transcend time and space — and be seen, heard or felt at any point in time. Superstring theory attempts to explain all of the particles and fundamental forces of nature in one theory, or a Theory of Everything. The implications of superstring physics are radically changing our ideas about the nature of space, opening up the possibility that extra dimensions, rips in the fabric of space and parallel universes actually exist.

Theoretical physicists also are excited about the existence of the Zero Point Field (ZPF), which may explain how everything that exists in the universe is connected to everything else. The ZPF is made up of Zero Point Energy (ZPE), virtual particles whose electromagnetic fluctuations fill every corner of space and are never at a state of absolute zero momentum, but instead vibrate at the most minute rate of oscillation allowable by the laws of quantum physics. Marie Jones, in her book titled PSIence: How New Discoveries in Quantum Physics and New Science May Explain the Existence of

Paranormal Phenomena, describes this vibration as "a tiny, residual jiggle." Jones explains that by virtue of the ZPF, reality is one big spider web with an infinite number of fine strands criss-crossing, intersecting and creating a wholeness that extends throughout time and space.

What implications do the existence of the ZPF and ZPE have on the validity of residual hauntings? According to Jones, the supposed recording of the energy of an event could take place in the ZPF, which can be compared to the Akashic Records of Edgar Cayce, upon which every memory, action, thought and thing was written. These imprints, or recordings, could have found a way to exist intact upon the ZPF, and those who see replays of past events could have found a way to tap into them. As a result, psychically inclined individuals may smell gunpowder, hear cannon fire and see flashes of gunfire while walking around Little Round Top, Culp's Hill or Devil's Den.

Theoretical physicists remain very busy in laboratories seeking answers to these quantum enigmas, but can paranormal field investigators document tangible evidence at places like Gettysburg that can help validate these theories as they relate to hauntings? If so, what do they need to be looking for, and what tools should they be using?

Paranormal investigators such as Joshua Warren, author and president of LEMUR (League of Energy Materialization and Unexplained Phenomena Research), approach paranormal field research in such a way as to best contribute to scientific inquiry. Warren's goal is to accumulate well-documented cases and create a database of hard evidence. "If ghosts are non-physical entities that aren't restricted to the known laws of physical matter," he supposes, "then by using the scientific method and creating a collective database, we may one day have enough data to isolate the patterns and correlations that will finally realize the essential conditions for spectral interactions to occur."

Obtaining this type of hard evidence requires taking as many environmental readings as possible when conducting field research. In fact, a basic arsenal of field equipment might include geomagnetic field meters, electromagnetic field meters, temperature gauges, ion detectors and more. Given the strange atmospheric conditions that seem to manifest when witnesses experience imprint hauntings and time slips, it seems only prudent to follow the advice Warren and other serious investigators: Go to great efforts to measure environmental conditions in an attempt to isolate the patterns and correlations associated with these phenomenon.

This photo was taken of a monument in the Rose Woods. Notice the sitting shadowy figure.

When conducting paranormal investigations, however, the best opportunities often occur when you least expect them, which is why being prepared at all times remains critical to the success of field research. For example, about five years ago while doing a field investigation at Gettysburg, a team psychic appeared very excited as she approached me in the Wheatfield. She said a portal had opened up in the Rose Woods (adjacent to the Wheatfield), but that she couldn't find me in time before it closed. Apparently, her psychic abilities enable her to see these portals appear, and she describes them as a disruption or ripple in the atmosphere. It's during these brief moments that she feels it would be most advantageous to take environmental readings and photographs because this is when paranormal activity "peaks through our dimensional veil."

I immediately thought it would be a great idea to walk around the battlefield with her — for hours or even days if necessary — until this phenomenon occurred again. It seems well worth the effort to be able to measure the particular vibrations, frequencies or electromagnetic fluctuations associated with these anomalies. I consider her experience a profound one and am still deeply disappointed I wasn't in her general vicinity when this supposed portal opened.

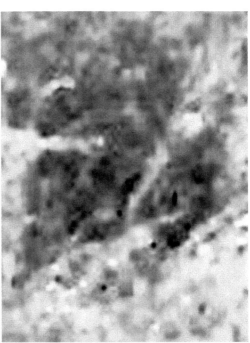

This photo was taken in the Wheatfield and reveals the head and shoulders of a ghost soldier crouching.

Could these portals represent the "rip in the fabric of space," the discontinuity in time, the warps or disruptions associated with superstring theory, or the manifestation of the Zero Point Field? And if one or more of these theories do apply to the phenomena reported at Gettysburg, what came first, the rabbit or the hole? Is Gettysburg located on or around an energy vortex or other cosmic quirk, thus exacerbating the frequency of hauntings in the area, or did the battle itself create the strong emotional imprints that somehow allow these quantum doors and windows to open up more frequently?

We can't know for sure at this point, but my intuition tells me that whatever this psychic detected is very important, and somehow these ripples in the atmosphere are the key to explaining at least some of the paranormal phenomena documented at Gettysburg and other battlefields across the globe. The answer is there, in front of us; we just need to know how to tap into its source, or essence, if you will.

— Jack Roth

CHAPTER 9 · SERENITY

"The soldier, above all other people, prays for peace,
for he must suffer and bear the deepest
wounds and scars of war."

- General Douglas MacArthur

Union earthworks on Culp's Hill.

Most paranormal experiences at Gettysburg are actually emotional in nature. Despite what many people believe, not all ghostly phenomena require audible sounds, physical manifestations or the capture of photographic evidence in order to represent a profound or noteworthy event. In fact, being affected emotionally by Gettysburg's energies — whether imprinted or spirit-triggered — tends to have a more-lasting impact on people. One can only imagine the intensity and range of emotions felt by more than 150,000 soldiers and 2,400 residents both during and after the battle. As such, it isn't difficult to understand how people can be "touched" emotionally while there.

While visiting Gettysburg with my wife Jean and my oldest daughter, Emily, we took a driving tour of Culp's Hill, a fairly sizable knoll with heavily wooded slopes. Culp's Hill was occupied by Union troops for just about the entire battle despite the best efforts of the Confederates to dislodge them. This area represented the point of the famous "fishhook" in the Union line often described by historians.

Jean has a degree in art history and has always been fascinated with history in general. Emily is much like her dad and finds military history to be fascinating. Jean is a sensitive, which loosely defined is a person who has a high degree of proficiency in extrasensory perception or can sense or feel paranormal events beyond the range of their five human senses. Although she possesses these abilities, she doesn't actively seek to exercise them. Regardless of her wishes, sometimes the ghost soldiers just don't care. Apparently, during our visit to Culp's Hill, a young soldier wanted her to know — and feel — what happened to him, and she had no choice in the matter.

As you start up Culp's Hill, the first stone wall you come to is where the 1st Maryland stood its ground for the Union during a ferocious Confederate attack on the second day of fighting. Right beyond this area on Slocum Avenue is where the 1st Maryland monument is located. As Maryland residents, we were very interested in checking out this site. I pulled the car over. Jean stayed in the car while Emily and I got out and approached the monument. We read each and every side of it, and I told Emily what it must have been like at this exact location on the day of the battle. We walked over to the earthworks that Union forces built to protect their strategic position on the hill.

When we got back to the car, Jean was very quiet and seemed taken aback. I asked what was wrong, and she told me the following story:

> *"I was just sitting here watching you and Emily walk around the monument and go over to the earthworks, and I couldn't help but think how awful it must have been. Men shooting, screaming and dying — it was quite overwhelming. Suddenly I felt all of that chaos leave my head, and a sense of peace came over me. I looked down at the ground and saw a young soldier lying between a small rock and a tree.*
>
> *"He was bandaged, but I knew he was dying ... yet he was at peace with this fact. All of the fighting seemed to melt away from him, leaving him in this small oasis of serenity. I said a silent prayer for him and then he was gone. Then I heard you and Emily coming back to the car."*

After Jean related her experience to me, I handed her my camcorder and she filmed the area in which she had the vision. There are times when a spirit wants to give you a glimpse of their life, a personal gift just for you. This was without a doubt one of those moments for Jean.

— Patrick Burke

CHAPTER 10 ~ ECHOES FROM THE PAST

*"Cry 'havoc!' and let loose the dogs of war,
that this foul deed shall smell above the earth.
With carrion men, groaning for burial."*

*- William Shakespeare,
"Julius Caesar"*

As we approached the Triangular Field on that cold, damp, misty morning, the only sounds that could be heard were the splatters of gentle raindrops deflecting off the moss-covered rocks and knee-high grass that saturated the landscape. It was 6 a.m., and the Gettysburg battlefield possessed a mystical quality, even more so than usual.

With heightened caution, we gingerly walked toward a wooden gate that acts as a landmark to where some of the bloodiest fighting took place in July 1863. We didn't want to trip and fall on the soggy ground, so we stepped slowly down a rugged path. We reached a large rock under which we had placed an infrared camera and microphone the night before. They were wet despite the protection of the tarps we left covering them.

"A casualty of field work," I thought, knowing that our technician would be less than pleased about the soaking of his equipment.

I carefully collected everything and handed it off to a fellow field investigator, who promptly took the equipment to the comfort of our heated car. We hoped the rain hadn't destroyed whatever anomalies we may have captured on tape.

I lagged behind, savoring the dreamlike atmosphere. I walked back up towards the wooden gate, thinking how great it felt to be on the battlefield without the usual hoards of tourists and busloads of noisy school kids. It was perfectly quiet, almost surreal. As peaceful as this felt, it was hard to believe that hell had once unleashed itself here.

And then I heard them …

The voices emanated from the bottom part of the Triangular Field by its northwest tree line. I initially deduced that I must have been hearing animals. I stopped in my tracks about 30 yards from the car in order to listen more carefully.

"Yip!"

"Hey!"

Silence for a few seconds and then more …

Muddled voices? Men screaming …

… coming up from the tree line toward where the Union line would have been holding ground …

"Yep!"

"Whoop!" "Whoop!"

Cows?

No way — maybe an angry farmer, but not cows.

School kids role-playing on the battlefield?

Not this early, and not in this weather.

I became unnerved.

I waited a few seconds to see if I could distinguish these sounds and pinpoint exactly where they were coming from.

They were getting closer, yet I couldn't see anything. Once more I heard distant screams …

"Yep!" "Yip!"

And then silence.

I waited a few minutes to make sure the sounds had subsided. At this point my fellow investigator opened the car window and stuck his head out.

"What's up?" he asked. "Did you hear something?"

"Yes. I think I did," I responded. "You're not going to believe this, but I think I just heard rebel yells …"

***

I documented the above account shortly after experiencing the phantom sounds, which seemed to originate from the very landscape on which I was standing. Since my strange auditory encounter, I've become fascinated with the Triangular Field, an area of the Gettysburg battlefield that seems to retain a great deal of residual energy.

Confederate General Longstreet

There are several historical facts that support what I may have heard on that misty morning. The Triangular Field has become synonymous with the death and destruction associated with the whole of the battle of Gettysburg. On the morning of the second day of fighting, Confederate Gen. Robert E. Lee believed that if he could simultaneously attack the Union flanks, he could drive the enemy from the field. Part of his plan was to send Gen. James Longstreet's 1st Army Corps southward to overrun the Union left flank anchored on Little Round Top. In order to even reach Little Round Top, the Confederates had to endure some of the bloodiest fighting of the battle in terrain now referred to as the Triangular Field and Devil's Den. Within just a few hours, thousands would be left either dead or wounded on these blood-soaked grounds.

As Confederate brigades under the command of Gen. John Bell Hood made their way southward, they came upon a sloping, triangular field. Waves of Confederate troops from Texas, Arkansas, Alabama and Georgia crossed this field, clashing with Union regiments from New York, Maine and Pennsylvania. The Confederate forces were initially cut down by Union artillery posted on top of a small ridge adjacent to the large boulders of Devil's Den, but the Confederates continued to push forward with repeated charges by the 15th Georgia and the 1st Texas Infantry. Shouting the famous rebel yell, the 1st

Texas charged up the Triangular Field to finally take the summit. The Georgians and Texans proceeded to overrun Devil's Den and took three Union cannons as prizes.

Alexander Hunter, a member of Longstreet's staff, later recalled how the rebel yell would adversely affect the enemy:

Did the wailing battle cries of Confederate infantrymen imprint themselves into the surrounding environment?

"When our reserve, led by Hood's Texas Brigade, the pride and

glory of the Army of Northern Virginia, came on a run, gathering up all the fragments of other commands in their front, and this second line clashed straight at the enemy, then I heard the rebel yell with all its appalling significance. I never in my life heard such a fearsome, awful sound. ... I have often dreamed of it; above the uproar of a great battle it dominated. On those charging columns of blue it had a decided effect, for it portended capture, mutilation or death and brought eternity very near."

Indeed, the rebel yell was a battle cry used by Confederate soldiers during charges to intimidate the enemy and boost their own morale. Union soldiers, upon hearing the yell from afar, would guess that it was either the Confederates about to attack or rabbits in distress, suggesting a similarity between the sound of the rebel yell and a rabbit's scream. The yell has also been likened to the scream of a wild cat, as well as similar to Native American war cries. One description says it was a cross between an "Indian whoop and wolf-howl." Although nobody has ever actually heard the cries of the fabled banshees from Greek mythology, the rebel yell has often been compared to these blood-curdling wails simply based on their disconcerting affects on those who hear them.

Given the differences in descriptions of the yell, there may have been several distinctive yells associated with the different regiments and their respective geographical areas. Another plausible source of the rebel yell is that it derived from the screams traditionally made by Scottish Highlanders when making a Highland charge during battle. This was a distinctive war cry of the Gael — a high, savage whooping sound.

A great deal of documented eyewitness testimony supports the existence of paranormal activity in the Triangular Field. Confederate sharpshooters have been sighted on the rocks down at the bottom of the field, at the end of the woods, as if preparing to shoot. Strange sounds have been heard, including screams described as rebel yells, emanating from either the wooded area to the right of the wooden gate or down at the bottom end of the field. Artillery blasts have also been heard, as well as the screaming and moaning of wounded and dying soldiers. Union soldiers have been sighted at the left of the gate entrance of the field and have even been known to approach visitors.

The Triangular Field

Suffice to say, the Triangular Field remains a focal point in our research at Gettysburg. Although perhaps no more haunted than any other part of the battlefield, the smaller, more enclosed nature of the field makes it an ideal place in which to set up a triangulation (no pun intended) of recording equipment, thus making full coverage of the field plausible. In the end, the range and frequency of paranormal activity experienced in this small field cannot be ignored.

— Jack Roth

CHAPTER 11 ~ ONE GALLANT RUSH

"Accurst be he that first invented war."

- Christopher Marlowe,
British dramatist

On July 2, 1863, Confederate Gen. Robert E. Lee intended to launch the Army of Northern Virginia in multiple attacks against the flanks of the Army of the Potomac and shear the Union defenses. Coordinated correctly, these "en echelon" attacks would force confusion in the Union lines and eventually breach it at its weakest point. Lee's plan was solid, but his lines were stretched out over a long distance, and coordination of the attack would become more difficult than he anticipated. Nevertheless, the day's fighting was fierce, inflicting catastrophic casualties on both sides.

I decided to visit the spot where Confederate Brigadier Gen. Cadmus Wilcox and his brigade of Alabamians stopped to realign before pushing to the top of Cemetery Ridge. I stood on the Confederate side of the approach to the ridge, looking at the 1st Minnesota Volunteer Infantry monument with its lone soldier in full stride, musket leveled. Staring at the monument, I thought what must have gone through the minds of the Confederate soldiers as they heard the Union huzza and saw the large number of Union soldiers come streaming out of the smoke towards them. And I marveled at the valor of the 262 men of the 1st Minnesota, a Union regiment that went into battle at the most critical time, when the Union center on this part of the field was crumbling, against a force that was six times its size. When the smoke cleared, only 47 men from the 1st Minnesota returned to their original line on Cemetery Ridge.

I've been told that valor is often born of circumstance. History tells us that Union Gen. Winfield Scott Hancock saw Wilcox's brigade, unchallenged, forming near the base of a ridge with the intent of charging a gap in the Union line. Hancock knew he needed reinforcements desperately and saw the 1st Minnesota close at hand. He pointed to a Confederate flag over the advancing line and shouted to Col. William Colvill of the 1st Minnesota, "Advance, Colonel, and take those colors!"

Union General Hancock

Colvill's task was critical. If he and his men couldn't delay Wilcox's brigade from penetrating the gap before more reinforcements arrived, the Confederates would most certainly push the Union forces off of their strategic position on Cemetery Ridge. If that happens, the entire Union line collapses, and the outcome of the battle is very different.

As I stood by the monument, an overwhelming sense of trepidation descended upon me. "Dear God! Plug the gap or all is lost!" Could these have been Hancock's thoughts when he first rode up the ridge and witnessed the desperate situation unfolding before him? Did I just trigger a residual haunting? The thought rang in my head and caused me to pause where I stood, looking back at the monument. The 262 men of the 1st Minnesota charged directly into the center of Wilcox's 1,700 Alabamians with a tremendous yell. The unit's flag fell five times and rose again each time. They momentarily stopped the Alabamans cold. Ten minutes later, the small group of surviving Minnesotans (47 men all wounded and exhausted) came streaming back as fresh Union troops came over the ridge and engaged Wilcox's brigade at the foot of the ridge. The 1st Minnesota's 83 percent casualty rate stands to this day as the largest loss by any surviving military unit.

As I stood there in awe of such bravery, a woman in her 40s came up beside me and started talking. She noted the logo on the back of my shirt and asked if I ever investigated this battlefield. I told her about some of the evidence we've captured and described some of the more personal moments I've experienced on the battlefield.

She then recounted the following story to me:

"I was walking in the early morning, just after sunrise, along the road just behind us. I enjoy taking brisk walks through the battlefield at that time in the morning because everything is so peaceful. As I approached the area we're standing in, I heard a great commotion. It sounded like a football game with a lot of people shouting. I couldn't see anyone around me, but it seemed to come from the area where that monument (she pointed at the 1st Minnesota monument) is standing. I moved closer to investigate when I heard a tremendous cheer from what seemed like hundreds of voices, and then suddenly the sounds were gone."

I asked her if she heard anything else, but she said she only remembered the shouting and especially that final cheer. It seemed so odd and out of place to her. I then described the cheer as a "hurrah" and asked her if that was close to what she heard. She believed it was. Did she hear the cry of the 1st Minnesota as they charged into history? Did she hear the subsequent cheers that came from the approaching Union reinforcements who witnessed their gallant rush? Did her being in the right place at the right time allow her to experience the "living history" of an emotional event that took place on this spot 148 years ago?

Often, the random individuals you meet while exploring Gettysburg have fascinating stories that they are more than willing to share with you. It seems they are drawn to the battlefield for one reason or another, whether they are a descendant of someone who fought in the battle or a witness to a strange paranormal event that keeps them coming back, they all have a tale to tell.

Sometimes, they represent solid eyewitnesses to paranormal phenomena, and it's important to document such stories in order to enhance the database of information that can help researchers develop patterns as to where and when certain phenomena take place.

I, for one, always return to the 1st Minnesota monument to see if I can witness (and capture) a part of the amazing events that took place more than 148 years ago. If nothing else, I'm happy to stand and honor the men who rushed in the face of great odds and willingly sacrificed their lives for a cause in which they believed so strongly.

– Patrick Burke

CHAPTER 12 - HIGH STRANGENESS ON SEMINARY RIDGE

"They will attack you in the morning and they will come booming — skirmishers three deep. You will have to fight like the devil until supports arrive."

- General John Buford, June 30, 1863

On May 8, 2004, we decided to set up a private midnight tour of Seminary Ridge for the investigative team and our guests. We had heard of many ghostly encounters in this area and wanted to see if we could have some of our own, plus we knew it would be very quiet and free of tourists at such a late hour.

Seminary Ridge was the site of fierce fighting on the first day of the battle. This was where Union Gen. John Buford's Cavalry Corps 1st Division held off Gen. Henry "Harry" Heth's (pronounced as "Heeth") superior Confederate infantry forces long enough for corps of Union infantry to arrive at Gettysburg. From a strategic standpoint, Buford's holding action enabled the Union army to ultimately hold the high ground west of town (the Round Tops and Cemetery Ridge), which played a key factor not only in the Union victory at

General Buford

Gettysburg, but in the subsequent chain of events that led to the

South's ultimate defeat. As a result, the fighting at Seminary Ridge will remain etched in history as a watershed moment that changed the tide of the Civil War.

The beautiful Lutheran Theological Seminary dominates the geography of Seminary Ridge, as it sits majestically on its crest. It was from its highest cupola where Buford, while trying to lead his troops from the field, climbed up periodically to assess a broader view of a very grave situation — pivoting constantly with binoculars to watch both his badly outnumbered cavalry division holding off the Confederates to the north and for any sign of Union Maj. Gen. John F. Reynolds I Corps arriving from either the south or west. Reynolds arrived with little time to spare, and the rest is history.

Our tour began peacefully enough, as our knowledgeable guide gave us a detailed description of both the Lutheran Seminary and the riveting events of the battle's first day. But then, as is often the case in Gettysburg, what had been an uneventful midnight stroll slowly transformed into an emotional whirlwind of high strangeness. After the tour ended and the excitement subsided, I decided to get everyone back to our hotel in order to lead a roundtable discussion while the night's "festivities" were still fresh in everyone's memories.

The following is the transcription of that roundtable discussion, followed by a brief discussion between two field investigators that was also documented.

Shannon: I was kneeling ... looking at the lady who was giving the tour and just looking up, and I saw a pinpoint of light streak over the top of her head.

Jack: How far above her would you say it was?

Shannon: Maybe 4 feet.

Jack: How far did it streak?

Shannon: Maybe a foot. I didn't see it for very long. After about a foot it just disappeared, so I figured it was a bug that had gone out of the line of the light hitting it.

Jack: What direction was it going? Was it coming towards you or away from you?

Shannon: It went from left to right over the tour guide's head.

Jack: Can you describe the light?

Shannon: It was more of a small pinpoint streaking across the sky.

Jack: How big would you say it was?

Shannon: not even an inch, which is why I first assumed it was a bug.

Sean: I think I saw the same thing at a different time. I didn't really think much about it. It was when she was talking about the widow's house, and I saw it 7 to 10 feet above her head, starting off at golf ball size and trailing about six feet. It was yellow and reddish. It got no bigger than a softball.

Jack: So what do you think it might have been?

Sean: Your guess is as good as mine.

Jack: Shannon, yours kind of sounds like it could have been a bug. Do you really think it was?

Shannon: I'm not sure.

Sean: But it wasn't a straight streak either. It was a little bit crooked, still going in the same direction, but never like, never dramatically changing, but it's still changing nonetheless. Kind of like that a little bit (motions with hand). So I wasn't quite sure. Maybe the light caught my eye funny or something, but you (to Shannon) happened to mention it, and everybody else mentioned it ... so after you all mentioned it I thought, "Well hey, maybe it's not me seeing things."

Jon: What I saw was different. I was looking at the structure above the building where they say Buford used the tower to look for approaching reinforcements, and I saw something. It was long, and it was thin, and it shot up and actually hit the tower. It was a light because the shadows on the top moved and changed position like somebody had just shown a light up there, and that's where it stopped. It didn't go through the other end, so I looked around thinking there was a bright searchlight in the area. Like from a police car, that's how bright it was. I started thinking that no light could shoot all the way up there to the top of that tower. So that's what I saw.

Jack: So did it seem to correlate with the time that everyone else saw the streak of light?

Jon: It was maybe within the first minute and a half of the tour guide's story. The light basically traveled from the area behind her, like if there was a police car or what I first thought was a park ranger's car.

Jack: What else did you all experience out there?

Todd: Debbie, when you were looking through the window at the Seminary, I walked over and I took a picture of the steps, and then I saw that you were looking in the window. So I decided to take a picture of you, and just as I lifted my camera I saw a light about 10 or 12 feet away on my right-hand side on the ground. And it wasn't the blue orbs that I've seen in your photos. This was something I've never seen in digital camera displays, but it was a light on the ground and then it was just gone. Something was definitely there and then it wasn't there, and it wasn't somebody else taking a picture because everybody else was standing at another location.

Jack: Could it have been a flashlight?

Debbie: It was just the two of us on that side, so no.

Todd: No. Nobody else was there. It was totally dark on that side of the steps and I didn't know she was there. I don't know why I walked over there. This is the first time I've done anything like this.

Jack: When the tour guide was talking about John Reynolds, obviously we were in front of her. We were looking around the street corner where those houses were, in the same direction she said they took Reynolds' body. I don't know if he was shot there, probably not, but at that point they were probably taking him off the battlefield to place his body in a house or store in town. Anyway, she was talking, going on about it, and I looked over and saw this white light moving towards the street corner. There was this big bush on the corner, so I saw this glowing form for about two or three seconds, and it was higher up ... it was probably about five or six feet off the ground. It happened really quickly. So I thought it might be a person walking with a bright white shirt. You know, that's what I assumed right away, and then I thought, "Let me see what happens when it turns the corner and comes out from the other side of the bush that was blocking my view" ... but it never did. I kept staring at the same location to make sure. I wanted to make sure nothing came out. Nothing ever came out. If a person was walking down the street, they would have eventually come out from the other side of the bush because that's where the street went. It was a glowing white light and it was really quick. I saw the light for about three seconds. I didn't say anything at the time because I just saw the same type of anomaly at Spangler's Spring earlier tonight, so I was like, "Wow, this can't be happening twice in the same night, especially since I've never seen that type of thing in all my years leading up to this investigation. I don't know what's going on here, but it's fascinating.

Jon: When we first arrived for the ghost tour I was standing to the side looking at something on Seminary Ridge, and it looked like a cat. It was oblong and black, maybe the size of a football. And it kind of bounded down the hill a little bit. There was this bushy shrub tree, and it went behind that and disappeared. I poked Jack and we walked down there to make sure it wasn't a cat or something in the tree. We actually walked down past the tree and there was nothing in the tree. There was nowhere for it to jump out, and I watched the tree the entire time.

Robin: We were standing by the church steeple, not the cupola building, but the one next to it. It was near the end of the tour, and I just had this feeling in my peripheral vision or something, like something was going to happen to my right. So I turned around, took a few steps away from the tour guide and thought I saw what appeared to be soldiers. It was just a couple of them at first moving between the trees. This is when Debbie (a sensitive) came over, probably out of concern. There was such a strong odor of gunpowder that my eyes started tearing. And it was so bitter cold that my camera froze. The batteries did not fail; the camera froze! The zoom lens wouldn't move and nothing would work. Debbie came over, which was comforting because when you're in the midst of something like that away from the group you want somebody around.

Debbie: I walked over to her because she was standing perfectly still, so I thought, "OK, something's going on," and I had the EMF meter so I thought, "I'll go over and see what's up." As soon as I started walking towards her, the closer I got to her, the colder it got. By the time I got in front of her, I could smell the gunpowder, and we're both sniffing the air and asking, "Well, what do you smell?" She's telling me she's smelling gunpowder and I'm smelling the same thing, so I kind of knew we weren't both hallucinating this strange odor, and it was freezing cold.

Robin: It was freezing!

Debbie: I mean it was cold to begin with, but this was a bone-chilling cold. This went right through your skin like a deep, frigid cold. And then we lost you guys for a bit and had to find you again, and as the tour guide was telling the story about the soldier who was accidentally buried alive, we were looking again at that same area because the other thing we had seen was two columns of white, kind of misty, floating material. And we both saw it.

Robin: Just coming up from the earth ... mist ...

Debbie: But it didn't belong there; it wasn't supposed to be there and it wasn't right ... there was no mist anyplace else. So then we were walking towards it, and the closer we got to that little grove of trees the colder it was getting. We stopped and just were kind of watching. And you could see deeper shadows, but they were definitely people-shaped shadows moving between the trees, and they were definitely moving.

A ghostly mist forms in McPherson's Woods, where heavy fighting took place on the 1ˢᵗ day of the battle.

Robin: Exactly.

Debbie: Robin could follow them further than I could, and I lost them after a little bit, but there were at least three or four of them.

Robin: At least. There was a group of three, and there was another pair of two, and there was another group of at least four. We were really careful to point out where and in what direction they were moving. Whether it was at the streetlight, to the right of the streetlight, or ahead of the tree. We were really careful to identify movement to each other to make sure we weren't seeing car tail lights or something like that.

Heather: Going back to the dark shadows, when we were walking I had to stop because my back was hurting, and in the corner of my eye I saw someone walking. Actually I thought it was Robin because it was a dark black figure and she was wearing black. I kind of looked and then I looked back, and all of a sudden I see Robin and Debbie all the way on the other side, so I'm like "OK, that wasn't her." And then as I thought about it, the way the shadow was moving was kind of like a strut, and that freaked me out because it looked very human.

Jack: Wow. A lot of mysterious shadows and lights. Anything else?

Jon: We got turned around on Seminary Ridge and wound up on Confederate Avenue, so we got to ride along where Pickett's division formed before Pickett's Charge and all the way down to the end of the Confederate line. I mean it's miles and miles of tree line and monuments and cannons and everything else, and as we drove down I saw a large rectangular light, a bright light out in the middle of the battlefield. It was distinctly purple and as large as one of the monuments. It was as if somebody put a purple film in front of a light to make the light change color. It was bright and purple, and it was basically lit up in the middle of the battlefield.

Jack: That's very strange. I was in the car with you guys but I was looking the other way when it happened. Both of your reactions were interesting, because you both reacted at the same time to whatever you saw.

Jon: Yes. That's right. Scott saw it too. As we rode by we were like, "What the heck was that?" and we had to turn a corner and go right past where it was. None of us saw it once we took the corner, and it just wasn't practical to turn back around to see if we could see it because we had people following us back here, but it was definitely there. We drove down towards it, and as soon as we made the left and rode past it, it was completely gone. It wasn't our headlights illuminating anything either, so it wasn't like it disappeared because our headlights went off.

Scott: Yeah, I saw it too. It was the weirdest thing. We tried to come up with a rational explanation of what it could have been, but we couldn't. It was one of the weirdest things I've ever seen. And why purple? It's been a very strange night.

Union dead next to McPherson's Woods.

The following are further details given by Scott and Jon after the roundtable discussion in an effort to learn more about the streaking light seen on Seminary Ridge:

Scott: We were standing out there just enjoying the tour. The tour guide had set down her lantern, and we were all gathered around in a semicircle. Suddenly, almost 30 feet above us, I saw a very intense, extremely bright white streak of light. It wasn't a ball of light casting a contrail; it wasn't any fixed thing. It was just like a stretch of light that was about three to four feet long. It started out about three or four inches wide and as it went along it stretched and elongated a little bit, and then it just dissipated. It kind of looked like a glowing surfboard, to be honest with you. So basically, it started about right here (motions to spot) about 25 feet above us and it went and kind of streaked this way (makes movement with arm). Other people who were with us saw strange lights as well.

The Lutheran Theological Seminary

Jon: I think I saw the other end of what Scott saw. When I first got to that spot, instead of listening to the tour I was watching the top of the Seminary to try and see if I could see anything up in the tower. I saw

ıнStop.

shadows up there move like somebody hit it with a flashlight, and I looked around to tell somebody but I didn't see anybody else looking that way, so I was going to wait until the end of the tour, but that's when I heard the others talking about seeing a light coming from over this way (motions with hands) then dissipate going this way (motions with hands). But that's what I saw. The tour guide also told us she saw the same thing happen about two or three times before we got there. Her husband saw it once and she saw it twice — a light from that general area streaking across the sky, but it never followed the same pattern twice. And there were no lighthouses or searchlights around there, so it couldn't have been that.

Scott: And what you saw was moving in the same trajectory as what I saw. But what I saw faded out, so it's almost like Jon was looking in a different direction and whatever it was kind of re-intensified later on down the line but at the same trajectory. There was another girl on our tour; she saw the exact same thing I did from the same perspective.

These interviews illustrate just how hard it is to accurately describe and define paranormal incidents. Each person who saw the streaking light on Seminary Ridge most likely saw the same thing but had a different interpretation of what it looked like. In this case, one person's bug was another person's ghostly surfboard. Different interpretations aside, notice how in a group setting as one person starts to open up about experiencing something, other people start to feel more comfortable about it and chime in with their own experiences. It started with a flash of light in the sky that Shannon thought might be a bug, but thankfully she wasn't afraid to mention it. From that we obtained compelling and corroborative testimony involving other strange lights, moving shadows, glowing figures, the overwhelming smell of gunpowder, shadowy soldier figures and a huge flash of purple light seen right where Pickett's men would have congregated to prepare for their famous charge. This is why having roundtable discussions (in a relaxed atmosphere) after a paranormal event represents an effective way to draw out and document eyewitness testimony.

That night on Seminary Ridge was one of the most interesting nights I've ever spent in Gettysburg, but what exactly did we see? Surprisingly, seeing flashes and streaks of light on the battlefield is more common than one might think. Some theorize these may represent the imprinted energies of both gun and cannon fire, which is certainly a plausible explanation considering the concentrated amount that was expelled in a three-day period. As for smelling the gunpowder, this too could easily represent a residual haunting, as the entire battlefield and surrounding countryside must have permeated with the smell of gunpowder (and other, much more ghastly things) for days. Regarding the shadows and the glowing figures, we'll probably never know; we obtained no photographic evidence to corroborate the visual sightings.

In the end, these experiences left us with more questions than answers, but by documenting them, we may someday be able to develop a viable blueprint as to the nature of paranormal activity. And perhaps more importantly, engaging in the pursuit of these answers allows us to witness profound events and learn a great deal about — if nothing else — the human experience.

— Jack Roth

CHAPTER 13 - GUT SHOT SOLDIER

"No history ever — no poem sings, no music sounds, those bravest men of all — those deeds. No formal general's report, nor book in the library, nor column in the paper, embalms the bravest, north or south, east or west. Unnamed, unknown, remain, and still remain, the bravest soldiers. Our manliest — our boys — our hardy darlings; no picture gives them."

- Walt Whitman, American poet

Do you see the soldier leaning against the "V-shaped" tree?

Sometimes you capture the most incredible paranormal evidence when you least expect it. As a case in point, a few years ago I was trying out my new Sony NightShot Plus camcorder and wanted to see how it would record when shooting at dusk in the near-infrared format. I decided to film at Spangler's Spring, partly because I'd never filmed there before and partly because of the time of day, around 7:30 p.m. The sun was setting behind the trees near the spring, which would help eliminate any direct sunlight that might cause the image to become completely overexposed as a result of too much light pouring into the lens aperture.

A natural spring that flows at the southern end of Culp's Hill, Spangler's Spring was a focal point for the wounded men, on both sides, during the Battle of Gettysburg (see Chapter 4: First Sighting). Drinking from the spring's refreshing water was, in some cases, the last pleasurable act many of these men experienced before dying. The fierce fighting that occurred on this area of the battlefield remains vastly underestimated, but many soldiers' recollections of the combat around Spangler's Spring vividly capture its true devastation. Union Col. George Cobham of the 111th Pennsylvania Infantry described the carnage in a letter he wrote to his brother on July 4, 1863.

"We have just concluded the most severe battle of the War, which has resulted in a complete victory on the Union side. The fighting has lasted two days and been desperate on both sides. All round me as I write, our men are busy burying the dead. The ground is literally covered with them and the blood is standing in pools all around me; it is a sickening sight."

Henry Hunt, Chief of Artillery in the Army of the Potomac, remembered the thick forest of hardwoods on Culp's Hill that bore the scars of the battle for many years afterward.

"The scene of this conflict was covered by a forest of dead trees," he wrote in the 1880's, *"leaden bullets proving as fatal to them as the soldiers whose bodies were thickly strewn beneath them."*

Should you have the chance to visit, imagine what it would

look like with hundreds of wounded men moaning and crying out for help. Imagine also the dead lying all around, their sightless eyes staring into the sky. If I had to choose one area on the battlefield that could provide witnesses with the best chance of experiencing a paranormal event, I would argue that Spangler's Spring is as good a place as any due to the immense suffering and bloodletting that occurred there in a relatively short period of time.

Spangler's Spring is one of the many paranormal hot spots on the battlefields.

I set the camcorder on a tripod and selected a spot just in front of the spring, filming a small band of Confederate reenactors who set up a small camp behind the boulders and tree's across from Spangler's Spring and the base of Culp's Hill. My daughter Emily was with me at the time, and I filmed her hiding, jumping and playing soldier for about three minutes. The camcorder worked great in the infrared mode at dusk. The picture possessed a slightly green tint, but otherwise the quality was excellent. Emily went over to talk with my wife Jean, who was waiting in the car, so I again focused on the reenactors. After several minutes of filming them going about their campsite routine, I moved the camera approximately 10 feet to my right and began shooting the area from a different angle.

As I always do when using cameras, I noted the activity in front of the camcorder. Emily was the only person in the frame's foreground, and four or five reenactors were in the background moving around the campsite. I had a feeling that something unusual was going to happen around them. In fact, I've found that reenactors can help facilitate paranormal events, and I've used them on a number of occasions when doing experiments during investigations. When I arrived back at our hotel room, I reviewed the tape and found what I expected (and hoped) I might capture — the full apparition of a gut shot soldier!

When we replayed the footage, the form of a soldier with his back to a forked tree and his body covering the bottom front of a large boulder could be clearly defined. It remained in view for almost three minutes. It appeared as if his feet were bootless and a dark mass covered his abdomen. I intuitively believed the dark mass indicated the area of his fatal injury.

Did a ghost soldier honor me with a glimpse of how he died at Gettysburg? Did his comrades make him as comfortable as possible before heading back into the fight? The footage still has a profound impact on me. It makes me wonder what were this soldier's last thoughts. Did he think about his wife, who waited nervously for him to return home? Did his thoughts drift to his children, who had probably grown so much since he left home to fight for the cause. Or, like so many of the very young boys who died on this battlefield and never got the chance to marry and have children, perhaps he thought about his mother and the sense of comfort and safety she always provided him.

I returned the next day and took some notes at the specific location where I captured the paranormal event. I noticed in the exact spot where the apparition appeared that no dark masses were present. No large concentration of moss or leaves existed, certainly nothing the size of the dark mass in the video. And there were no logs, bushes or tree branches in front of the boulder that could be mistaken for a person.

I knew what I captured was real and that this soldier "allowed" me to capture him on videotape, but how can I explain and make sense of it? Often on battlefields, when you visit with an open mind and heart and respect the sacrifices of the soldiers who fought there, you begin to establish a connection of sorts with the energies that remain behind. I can't describe why this happens, but I can say it represents the most fulfilling part of what I do. I'm capturing moments in history. I'm like a bard of old, a traveling storyteller who is privileged to have experienced special connections and who shares the stories of the fallen brave in their own words.

– Patrick Burke

CHAPTER 14 ~ HIGH, LOW AND PRETTY MUCH ALL OVER

"What the horrors of war are, no one can imagine. They are not wounds and blood and fever, spotted and low, or dysentery, chronic and acute, cold and heat and famine. They are intoxication, drunken brutality, demoralization and disorder on the part of the inferior ... jealousies, meanness, indifference, and selfish brutality on the part of the superior."

- Florence Nightingale

Dead Confederate soldiers in the Slaughter Pen.

Plum Run Creek, also known as Bloody Run, is a small stream that runs through a gorge known as the Valley of Death. This valley is located between Devil's Den and Little Round Top, which made it a natural clashing point during the battle of Gettysburg. The creek earned its infamous nickname after it ran red with the blood of fallen soldiers, mostly Confederates who were trying to overrun Little Round Top. On July 4, 1863, one day after the battle ended, heavy rains caused the creek's shallow banks to overflow, and several Confederate wounded, who couldn't move and had not yet been retrieved by their comrades, drowned tragically. Veterans of the battle described the valley surrounding Plum Run as littered with so many bodies that it took over a week after the battle ended for all of the fallen men to be buried.

It all started at approximately 5 p.m. on July 2, 1863, when Union Brig. Gen. Samuel W. Crawford moved two of his Pennsylvania infantry brigades forward across the Valley of Death (which subsequently garnered the nickname the Slaughter Pen) against approaching Confederate infantry who were attempting to reach the summit of Little Round Top and flank the Union left. Between the 2nd U.S. Sharpshooters, who were stationed behind an insulating stone wall at the base of the hill, and Union Capt. James Smith's remaining cannons from his 4th New York Battery, severe casualties were inflicted on Rebel infantry from both the 2nd Georgia regiment advancing along the creek, and the 4th and 5th Texas and 15th Alabama regiments advancing towards the open south side of Little Round Top. The Valley of Death and Plum Run Creek became an inferno of gun and cannon fire, resulting in high casualties and forever entrenching these geographic landmarks into the tragic lore of the battlefield.

Early one evening in the spring of 2004, while investigating Devil's Den, a young couple in our group looked out of their car and saw what they described as bright flashes of light appearing randomly above the tree line just beyond Plum Run Creek. Most orb-like phenomena tend to be photographic in nature and are very controversial, but the fact that they saw these lights with the naked eye makes this a more unique encounter. It was a very clear night, and they were able to watch these flashes of light for approximately three minutes as they appeared to move lower and closer to them as time went by. As is often the case when witnesses have the time to carefully analyze what they are seeing, they were able to rule out some mundane possibilities. They stand by their testimony and remain adamant that these lights were not car or plane lights, flashlight reflections, shooting stars or fireflies (a.k.a. lightning bugs).

I documented their description of the lights immediately, and we stayed around Plum Run Creek for a while in the hopes of seeing the lights again. The lights did not return, but the witnesses managed to take digital photographs while observing them, and as a result captured glowing anomalies on just about every one of their shots. No details could be discerned from the photographs, but they did confirm the validity, and location, of the sighting. Following is their testimony:

Eric: It was probably around 9:30 p.m., around that time frame, and we were over by Devil's Den. We were parked down further to the right of the last few spots if you were looking down at the parking lot from the big boulders. Almost everyone from our group was back on the other side of the parking lot heading over towards Little Round Top. There was also a bunch of other people who were walking up towards the top of Devil's Den ... moving up the hill with flashlights. We decided to stay down more towards the woods near the creek because it was much quieter down there.

Tammy: We also got back into the car because we were cold.

Eric: We were just kind of hanging out, and it was pretty dark over in that spot and we started noticing some flashes of light kind of up high over the tops of the trees.

Tammy: They were up high in the sky, way above the treetops at first.

Eric: It occurred to me right away that there could be a road back behind the wooded area and that we could be seeing car lights flashing through the trees as the cars drove by, but we ruled this out and then we thought maybe it was a plane, a low flying plane, and that we were seeing its lights blinking as it flew behind the trees. But that just wasn't right; it didn't fit the description because a plane never came into view, and the lights didn't flash in a line. They were random in nature.

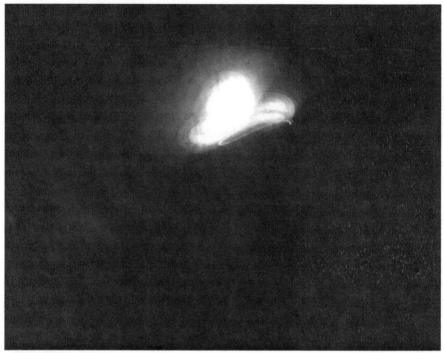

This flash of light was captured against the trees at Plum Run Creek.

Tammy: They covered a pretty wide area above the trees.

Eric: At first they were up high. Right after we ruled out car or plane lights, we started seeing more flashes down low, and much closer to us.

Tammy: They were high, low and pretty much all over, which was just very strange because they didn't seem to look like any lights we had ever seen. They were more like star bursts than anything else.

Jack: Could they have been the flashlights from the other people who were climbing up the rocks at Devil's Den?

Tammy: No way. These lights were way too bright, and they didn't move like someone was moving a flashlight around. I can say with certainty they weren't flashlights.

Eric: Right, and they were all over, so we were able to rule out the plane theory and the flashlight theory right away. Then the last thing that occurred to us was that they might be lightning bugs, you know, fireflies, but again it wasn't a good explanation. These lights were much brighter and bursting.

Tammy: Yeah, they weren't really floating around like fireflies do.

Eric: They weren't pulsating as much as they were flashing. In other words, there was no dimming up and down, just very quick flashes. You couldn't see any kind of pulse like you would see from a lightning bug. And right about the time we ruled out just about everything "normal" it could be, they started really flashing all around us.

Tammy: These flashes were all over the place, and now I started to get very intrigued because they were moving closer to us. Not scared at all, but very excited.

Eric: Tammy jumped out of the car with the digital camera and started snapping a few photographs, and from what we can tell right at first glance there are some round circular lights that showed up in them.

Tammy: They appear in every picture I took, so they were definitely there.

Eric: Some are far away in the photograph, but one in particular seems really close to us, so we'll have to check those out more carefully.

Tammy: It was so cool, because your intuition just tells you these things were not natural. They seemed other-worldly.

Eric: This is our first paranormal investigation, and it's the first time we've ever experienced something like that. It was very fun, very cool.

Tammy: I would love to come back at 9:30 tomorrow night and see if we can see the same thing. Maybe it's time-related somehow.

Eric: Yeah. We would love to do that.

Jack: We'll definitely do that, and I'm glad your first experience was such a positive one. I wanted to ask you a question regarding how you felt as this was happening. Did you feel strange, or did you feel like the atmosphere around you changed at all?

Eric: Well, we were in the car at first, but the windows were open, and then of course we got out to take pictures as the lights got closer, but it's funny you ask that, because as time went by, it seemed as if everything else around us didn't exist. I can't recall any sounds, natural or man-made, so maybe I was just very focused on the lights. I can't speak for Tammy.

Jack: I ask this because sometimes people experience what is known as the Oz Factor, which is when the environment actually changes as you're experiencing a paranormal event. The atmosphere becomes different to people, and it's very hard to explain.

Tammy: I felt strange, but Eric and I were talking to each other, so that interaction was real. The lights themselves were strange, though. They seemed not-of-this-world, so to speak. I think you can just tell when something isn't right.

Jack: Yeah, that's why I ask that. We can examine your photographs on a computer when we get back to the bed and breakfast, but let's hang out in this area for a while and see what else might happen.

Eric: What happened in this area that may explain these lights ... paranormally, not naturally?

Jack: Soldiers were fighting all throughout this area and many of them died in this creek. But there was a lot of gun and cannon fire, which might explain these lights as a residual phenomenon. Many people see flashes of light all over this battlefield, and they aren't all fireflies, I can tell you that. It makes sense, but only if you believe residual hauntings are possible.

Tammy: I can see that for sure.

Eric: They did look like flashes of gunfire in the dark. That would be the most accurate description yet. Wow. I can really see that, but why high above the trees at first?

Jack: I can't say for sure, but certain kinds of artillery fire did explode above the trees, raining down shrapnel over the enemy. We can never know for sure, but I think your experience tonight was a really good one.

I still think about Tammy and Eric's experience for several reasons. First and foremost, they were really cool people and made for outstanding eyewitnesses. They weren't flaky and really performed an objective analysis regarding what they saw as they saw it, which should be commended. Also, my intuition tells me they saw something truly paranormal in nature. Usually, lights and orbs represent incredulous evidence at best, but when they are seen by more than one witness, for a prolonged period of time, with the naked eye, and appear in a way that defies all logical explanations, then such an event should be taken seriously and documented thoroughly.

The location factor also comes into play in this instance. Bloody Run, the Slaughter Pen, Devil's Den — these places are bathed in a history of bloodshed, emotional trauma and loss of life, and this must be taken into account when examining evidence or eyewitness testimony, especially when such evidence imitates the natural phenomena associated with the actual battle (gun flashes, cannon fire bursts, etc.).

For me, the best part of this story remains the fact that Tammy and Eric had what they truly believed was a real paranormal experience, and it was a positive and exciting one. We will probably never know what they saw that night, but I remain very happy for them because they experienced something special. Experiences like theirs often urge people to become more involved in paranormal research. I sincerely hope they continue to show an interest in investigating paranormal phenomena and approaching it in such an objective, logical manner. I for one believe they would make great field researchers.

— Jack Roth

JACK ROTH & PATRICK BURKE

CHAPTER 15 ~ PHANTOM CAVALRY RETREAT

"It is well that war is so terrible; else we would grow too fond of it."

- General Robert E. Lee,
December 15, 1862

On July 3, 1863, the third and final day of fighting in Gettysburg, Gen. James Ewell Brown "Jeb" Stuart's Confederate cavalry attempted to drive a dagger into the backs of the unsuspecting Union soldiers. Most people think of Pickett's Charge when they talk about the third day's action, but what's not so well known is the fact that Confederate Gen. Robert E. Lee had devised a more complex strategy to win the battle and capture most of the Army of the Potomac in the process.

As part of Lee's attack

General Stuart

plan, Gen. Isaac Trimble's North Carolinians would strike the left flank and part of the center of the Union line on Cemetery Ridge while Gen. George Pickett's Virginians struck the center of the line. The extreme left and right flanks of the Confederate forces would demonstrate along their respective fronts to keep all of the Union forces focused away from the main thrust of the approaching rebels. Stuart was ordered to take his cavalry and strike the rear of the Union defenses, thereby disrupting their line of communications while Pickett and Trimble hammered them from the front.

The plan was brilliant and aggressive, and it might have worked if it wasn't for an observant Union Gen. David Gregg, who heard cannon fire and caught sight of a company of Confederate cavalry. He rode close enough to see that it was a lead element of a much larger force. Indeed, Stuart's cavalry was heading towards the 3rd Pennsylvania Cavalry, which was set as a screen for the artillery reserve. Gregg quickly rode towards his commander's headquarters to alert him of the situation and get more cavalry support. While doing so, he came across two regiments of Union Gen. George Armstrong Custer's Michigan Brigade, who had recently been issued Spencer repeating rifles. These repeating rifles represented a significant tactical advantage during the Civil War, as they could fire 20 rounds per minute. Standard muzzle-loaders, on the other hand, could only fire two to three rounds per minute.

Custer was headed to the far left of the Union line as a screening force when Gregg approached and apprised him of the situation. At first Custer said he couldn't waiver from his orders, but Gregg assured Custer he would take full responsibility for the action if he would only divert his brigade to aid the 3rd Pennsylvania. Custer finally agreed and arrived on the field just in time to join the gallant charge.

As Confederate Gen. Fitzhugh Lee (nephew of Robert E. Lee) led the Confederate charge, the 3rd Pennsylvania Cavalry smacked into the center flank of the rebel cavalry, and Custer drove his cavalry directly at the front of the

General Custer

column of Confederate troopers. "Come on, you Wolverines!" Custer shouted. Seven hundred men fought at point-blank range with carbines, pistols and sabers. The Confederates were eventually overwhelmed and forced to retreat.

I decided to visit this part of the battlefield for the first time in July 2006 with ABGHS team members Mike Hartness and John Burke. As the night progressed, a strange feeling came over John and me near the Michigan and Pennsylvania monuments. The energy was high and a sense of foreboding hung in the air. As we got closer to the Confederate positions, the energy began to feel muddy, more depressed than the normal "bring it on" energy I usually feel when confronted with Confederate spirits.

We stood by a road that splits the woods where Fitzhugh Lee initiated his charge and where the Confederate cannons were placed. The atmosphere was heavy, and we spoke in hushed tones — the rebel ghost soldiers obviously having a direct effect on us. As we walked along the road with the woods to our left (in a direction that would take us away from Custer's Michigan Brigade), we heard the sounds of walking and movement in the woods. We immediately stopped and listened closely as the commotion continued. It sounded like both men and horses walking.

Mike walked over to the edge of the woods as John and I looked on. The sound grew fainter and finally stopped abruptly. When Mike came back, I asked him if he saw anything. He said no, but heard the sounds very clearly — men and horses moving away from the battlefield. Had we just experienced a residual haunting, hearing the imprinted energies of the actions that took place after Stuart's failed cavalry charge? Were the depressed feelings John and I felt those of the Confederates as they streamed back in defeat?

If you ever have the chance to go to the East Cavalry Field, you should do so. And when you're hanging out at the Michigan monument, ask the Union soldiers what they thought of Custer and if he was a hard commander. You might be surprised by the reply you get!

– Patrick Burke

CHAPTER 16 ~ CHAOS AND CARNAGE

"What the horrors of war are, no one can imagine. They are not wounds and blood and fever, spotted and low, or dysentery, chronic and acute, cold and heat and famine. They are intoxication, drunken brutality, demoralization and disorder on the part of the inferior ... jealousies, meanness, indifference, selfish brutality on the part of the superior."

- Florence Nightingale,
Crimean War Battlefield Nurse

The treeline at the edge of The Wheatfield where the ghostly head of a soldier appeared.

On the afternoon of July 2, 1863, a 20-acre field of wheat on the John Rose farm became the stage for some of the most vicious and costly fighting associated with not only the battle of Gettysburg, but of the entire Civil War. Although golden wheat grew tall on hundreds of other fields across southern Pennsylvania around the time of the battle, this patch of land would forever become known as the "Bloody Wheatfield," somehow delegating all other wheat fields to secondary status.

In the summer of 1863, the Wheatfield was surrounded by wood lots owned by the John Rose family. A small road and a large patch of land known as Trostle's Woods snaked its northern border. A worm-rail fence bordered its western edge, separating it from Rose Woods and a rocky knoll known as the Stony Hill. A stone wall separated the field from the section of Rose's Woods that stretched along its southern edge. Immediately to the east of the field was Houck's Ridge and Devil's Den, and beyond that Little Round Top, the ultimate prize for the Confederates, who attacked the Union defenses like a series of tidal waves on the second day of fighting.

Positioned at a relatively secure location on Cemetery Ridge on the morning of July 2, Gen. Sickles believed he saw higher ground ahead of him and advanced his entire Corp without orders, exposing the Union's left flank. His lines now stretched through fields far in front of those chosen by the Union's commanding general, George Gordon Meade. One such area along this new line was the now-infamous 20-acre field of wheat.

In the late afternoon, Confederate forces began their coordinated assault against Union lines beginning at its southern most point at Devil's Den and Little Round Top. As Southern brigades advanced in the direction of the Wheatfield, they were completely unaware that Union Gen. Daniel E. Sickles, the commander of the Army of the Potomac's Third Corps, had advanced his men to this location. In fact, the fighting in both the Wheatfield and the Peach Orchard actually occurred by accident — the result of Sickles ill-advised and unauthorized tactical maneuver (see Chapter 17: Fight or Flight).

At 4:30 p.m., when Confederate Brig. Gen. George T. Anderson's Brigade of Georgians and the 3rd Arkansas emerged from the Rose Woods and collided with Union brigades from the Third Corps in the Wheatfield, a melee of epic proportions began. Chaos ensued with a series of confusing attacks and counterattacks by 11 brigades from both sides, resulting in heavy casualties. In what must have seemed like utter pandemonium for the soldiers involved, the field changed hands six times in two hours.

By 7:30 p.m., the battle of the Wheatfield was over. The wheat lay trampled and the ground left soaked in blood with the dead and wounded stacked three and four deep. The casualty rates appalled even the most hardened of commanders. The 61st New York lost 60 percent of its number, all killed and wounded. The 53rd Pennsylvania lost 59 percent of its number. The 17th U.S. lost 58 percent. The Union regiments averaged losses of approximately one-third, with the Confederate regiments averaging about the same. In total, the Union suffered casualties of 3,215 and the Confederates 1,394. More than 4,000 men were killed or wounded in just over two hours of fighting. Some of the wounded managed to crawl to Plum Run but couldn't cross it. The river ran red with their blood, earning it the nickname "Bloody Run."

A New York soldier described the aftermath of the day's carnage:

"Silence followed the roar and tumult of battle. Through the darkness the rifles of the distant pickets flashed like fire flies, while, nearer by, the night air was burdened with the plaintive moans of wounded men who were lying between the lines and begging for water."

As one might expect, the Wheatfield represents a great location in which to conduct paranormal research. On May 8, 2004, our investigative team conducted a daytime experiment designed to cover the entire 20-acre field. We performed a grid-like walkthrough with several participants. The "sweepers" spread out approximately 15 yards apart and began walking across the field in unison from southern to northern edge. They each possessed handheld equipment in the form of still and/or video cameras, voice recorders, ion detectors and EMF Meters. Simultaneously, we set up video cameras along the higher elevations in order to capture various bird's eye views of the entire field.

I monitored the walkthrough with a walkie-talkie from the southern edge of the field while Jon, a fellow investigator, monitored the experiment with another walkie-talkie from the northern edge of the field. We did this so each sweeper could make at least one of us aware of an anomalous event, and we could then coordinate the movements of the entire team to the point of interest. Once they all reached the northern edge of the field, Jon would send them back through for a reverse walkthrough.

It was a beautiful day with temperatures in the mid-70's, low humidity and partly cloudy skies. Within seconds of beginning the experiment, a participant named Todd yelled aloud in excitement that he saw something. We hurried to his location and recorded his account.

Todd: I guess there were six or seven of us crossing the field. I was the first person from the western edge tree line and probably 15 yards from the edge. I was about 40 yards into it when from my right-hand side I saw a light traveling to the left towards the tree line.

Jack: Can you describe it?

Todd: I didn't see or sense anything but I saw a light, just a pure white light that was three or maybe four feet long and approximately eight to 10 inches in diameter. But I deal a lot with animals and I know it definitely wasn't any kind of animal. It was about a foot and a half off the ground and a bit higher than the grass, and it was traveling from right to left towards the tree line. I was on the left hand side, and when I saw it I didn't have time to take a picture because it was moving so fast.

Jack: Did it move in a straight line?

Todd: No. It went and circled around a large rock in a collection of rocks that were in the tree line and then it was just gone. It was really quick, instantaneous, and it definitely wasn't an animal.

Jack: Have you ever seen anything like it before, or was it completely unique to you?

Todd: I can't explain what it was. I never... this is the first time I've ever seen anything like this. It was definitely there, and it was a light about three or four feet long and eight to 10 inches wide.

Jack: Do you know where its point of origin might have been?

Todd: It seemed to just come out of the grass at a point west of my line. I thought it was being disturbed in some way as we all walked closer to it, and it disappeared into the tree line there, moving out of the field very quickly.

Jack: Was it easy to see in the daylight?

Todd: It was very clear, and very bright. And it was just very, very fast, shooting into the woods.

Jack: Could it have been a reflection of something hitting the sunlight?

Todd: This was a solid, bright, white light. It wasn't a bird or any animal I've ever seen before. It was luminescent, too big to be a bug and too fast to be a bird. I wouldn't have yelled out if it didn't register as something really out of the ordinary.

Considering what Todd just witnessed, we decided to focus our efforts on the wooded area on the western edge of the field where he witnessed the light vanish. We took readings and photographs along the edge of the tree line and slowly made our way into the woods. After only a few minutes, another participant, Rebecca, approached Jon and me with a look of horror on her face. She was pale and literally shaking, and we attempted to calm her down. Once she reached a decent state of calm, we recorded her testimony.

Jack: Can you tell us what happened?

Rebecca: We were all walking around looking for the light Todd saw. I went off to the right towards the very edge of the woods and climbed up those rocks and stepped over that fallen tree to the right. I was just standing very, very still at that point trying to get an electromagnetic reading. Debbie was about 50 feet or so to my left. I think she was trying to get some EVP.

Debbie: I was trying to get some EVP, but I also took some photographs.

Rebecca: I was standing there with the meter just being very quiet and I looked up, and about eye level with me or maybe a little above I saw a face. It was very solid and very clear. It was a man's face. He had dark hair, very heavy thick hair, full facial hair that was very dark, black almost, and then he locked eyes with me.

Jon: Where was he exactly?

Rebecca: He was by that tree, but just his face though. I couldn't see a body.

Jack: Did he look like a soldier?

Rebecca: Very much so. He had the kind of facial hair that was very common during the Civil War. And his face looked dirty.

Jack: Did he have a hat?

Rebecca: No. Not that I could see.

Jack: What did you do?

Rebecca: This is the first time I ever saw anything like this. The last thing I thought of was grabbing my camera. I just stared back at him trying to decide if I was really seeing what I thought I was seeing, and when I could finally breathe again I tried to motion for someone without speaking, you know, like "Come here!" because I didn't want to look away from him yet. But nobody saw my gestures. I locked eyes with this guy for what seemed like an eternity, and I finally looked over and everybody was gone.

Jon: Where were we?

Rebecca: You were there, but you all had walked in the other direction and I was kind of on the northern edge of the tree line. So I looked back, and he was gone. I actually stayed there looking for some more to see if it could've been a shadow or a configuration of shadows, or something that I could've mistaken, but I never found it again.

Jack: It's great that you did that. Let's walk over and check out the exact spot. Was he threatening?

Rebecca: It was very definitely a man and he was very mean. It was not a pleasant experience and it scared the heck out of me because he was very, very hostile. I just couldn't breathe when it happened. I just couldn't even breathe and you know when you feel tingly all over? Well that's how I felt. It was a very negative experience. He was just mean-spirited; at least that's how he came across to me.

Jack: OK. Well, he's gone now and you're safe with us. Do you mind showing us the exact spot?

Rebecca: No, as long as you guys are with me.

Debbie: You might want to check out this photograph I took of the tree line around the same time Jan had her experience. I sensed something by this tree, so I just snapped a shot and got this.

This daylight orb was captured by the treeline minutes after being seen in the Wheatfield. (Courtesy of Debbie Estep)

We checked Debbie's photo, and we were amazed to see a

white, glowing orb about the size of a large grapefruit or a small soccer ball to the left of the tree. It was located in the same area of the woods where Todd saw the glowing object enter the tree line and about 20 yards south of where Rebecca saw the man's face. Debbie's photo was taken during the day, in good lighting conditions, which rules out the often-misidentified dust particles that tend to illuminate when digital shots are taken in low-light conditions (which they usually are) and the flash goes off. The unique nature of the photo stems from the fact that such clear and pronounced glowing orb manifestations captured in daylight hours are quite rare. Let's not forget that Debbie also sensed something by the tree, which prompted her to take the photo in the first place. Therefore, her psychic intuition becomes a corroborative factor in this instance.

We also examined the area where Rebecca saw the face and saw nothing in the environment that could have resembled what she described to us. We did this in order to rule out *pareidolia* or matrixing, which is the phenomenon of seeing a familiar shape or form in random combinations of shadows and light. The shape or form itself is called simulacrum. One of the primary functions of the human mind is to make order out of chaos. Therefore, we have a tendency to see what looks like a face or familiar form in jagged rocks, dirt, water, clouds and even flames. The outdoor environment in Gettysburg is lush with trees, bushes, rocks, water sources and foliage in various stages of decomposition, and these combinations of shapes and forms often can be mistaken for soldiers, horses, guns and other elements associated with the battle.

What is extremely compelling about this series of incidents in the Wheatfield is the fact that three witnesses experienced profound phenomena, within minutes of each other, all of which can be linked in a logical manner. Let's recap: The first person (Todd) sees a visual sighting of an orb-like object streaking across the Wheatfield; the second person (Rebecca) experiences a harrowing apparitional sighting of a man's face in the same area where the orb-like object is last seen; and the third person (Debbie) senses something and takes a photograph of a similar orb-like object in the exact location where the first streak of light apparently enters the woods.

In the world of paranormal field research, this is known as a "big deal." When it comes to mostly non-tangible and non-replicable phenomena such as ghosts, science refuses to even consider their validity. Corroborative evidence represents the best validation of the phenomena we currently have at our disposal.

Could these anomalies be associated with the energies of one or more of the thousands of souls who lost their lives in the Wheatfield during the most epic battle of the war? We may never know for certain, but when solid eyewitness accounts of ghostly phenomena are encountered in an area where extreme emotional trauma took place in such a short period of time, it makes further study in and around the Wheatfield worthy of our time and effort.

– Jack Roth

CHAPTER 17 - FIGHT OR FLIGHT

"Anyone who has ever looked into the glazed eyes of a soldier dying on the battlefield will think hard before starting a war."

- Otto Von Bismarck, Prussian statesman

Dead Horsed on The Trostle Farm

Just behind the Peach Orchard lies the Trostle Farm, one of the areas where Confederate Gen. James Longstreet's forces clashed with

Union Gen. Daniel Sickles Third Corps on the second day of the battle. The fighting in this area was vicious, and it was the result of a bold salient — a maneuver that projects into the position of the enemy — made by Sickles that almost jeopardized the entire Union army. Sickles — a controversial, flamboyant and charismatic officer — didn't like the unfavorable nature of his original position on Cemetery Ridge and decided to move his troops forward towards the Peach Orchard to meet the enemy head on. Not only did Sickles disobey a direct order by Maj. Gen. George Gordon Meade to hold his ground, he exposed both sides of the Third Corps to enfilading fire and overextended the Union line.

General Sickles

As Sickles directed his forces in front of the Trostle Farm on a slight rise in the landscape, he could see the battle developing, but before he could meet the incoming Rebels, he was struck in the right leg by shrapnel. Being an old warhorse, Sickles told his aides to place a tourniquet on his leg and continued to direct his troops for several more minutes before being carried off the field. His leg was later amputated; a result that many officers believed saved him from being court-martialed for his rash and perilous action.

As the Confederate juggernaut pressed forward and Sickle's troops began to crumble, Union forces continued to rush men in to fill the gaps in their lines. The fighting around the Trostle Farm was intense, and many visitors to the battlefield have reported paranormal activity in that area. On a July night in 2006, a group of us made plans to meet at Gettysburg for an investigation. Ed Dubil, Jr. (Little Ed) and his dad (yup, Big Ed) wanted to do some ghost hunting around the Trostle Farm and the Peach Orchard, so we met there. We were all happy to have Brutus, Little Ed's ghost hunting dog, with us. This was the first time I had the chance to work with Brutus, and it turned out to be an incredible experience.

As a sensitive, I usually get a feel for the presence of ghost soldiers before most other people. My brother John and Big Ed were at the front and to the left of the barn as you face it from the Peach Orchard. Along the shoulder of the road, they set up two tripods with Sony "night-shot" camcorders as they talked about the various places they had investigated. Ed, Brutus and two close friends of mine, Chris Carothers (a talented sensitive) and Karen Mitchel (a rocket scientist … seriously!) joined me on the backside of the barn, standing near the area where wounded soldiers were cared for during and after the battle. Ed and I were talking about some of the experiences he had with Brutus and his father on the battlefield, and he recounted this story for me:

We were at the 11th Pennsylvania Infantry monument on Oaks Hill. The 11th had a mascot, a dog named Sally. Dad and I had been there before and never got any evidence, but on this overcast morning we decided to make another visit. Brutus did what all dogs do, checked out the area and then lay down near the statue of Sally. Dad wondered off videotaping while I began taking random pictures with my camera and turned on my digital recorder, placing it on the monument near the statue of Sally. No one else was there, just Dad, Brutus and me. As I normally do when on the battlefield, I thought about what it must have been like during the fighting, and also about the men who survived and went back to search, not only for their fallen comrades, but for Sally too. She had been missing since they retreated on July 1st. I imagined the relief they must have felt when they saw Sally, looking a bit sickly but alive, guarding their dead comrades. Suddenly Brutus sat up, his ears perked and his breathing very still, and then he trotted over to me. Later that night as Dad and I were going through the photos and videos, I played the recorder and all was quiet. All you could hear was my camera taking a few shots, that is until we heard a whistle and a man's voice calling out, "Here boy!"

As we walked toward the paved road that cuts through the Peach Orchard and past the barn, we could see John and Big Ed about 175 feet away, near their stationary cameras. I felt a sense of urgency as I watched Brutus stop, raise his ears and seem to hold his breath. I asked little Ed what Brutus was doing, and his response was, "It's called fight or flight. He is deciding if what he hears is a threat and, if so, can he win." Little Ed squatted down behind Brutus and took a photo between the dog's ears. The photograph revealed an orb about a foot away from where Brutus was standing.

As we walked around the barn to the spot were Sickles lost his leg, Chris (the sensitive) began to feel nauseated and confused. There was definitely a sense of dread around us, which I associated with the Union soldiers as they struggled to hold their position against overwhelming odds.

And then, suddenly, I heard the rebel yell. All around me it seemed like men were running, "Dear God," I thought, "this is how it felt to be on the receiving end of that howl!" Brutus' ears were up and his body was tense. Chris, Karen and Little Ed had moved about 50 feet away from me, and they showed no signs of hearing anything at all … and then the moment was gone.

A few days later my brother John called me and said he believed he had captured a mass of men rushing past the barn towards the Peach Orchard. When we reviewed the footage together, we could see (although the quality of the video is lacking) a mass of shadows crossing between the fence rails and the barn, and we could even see the shadow of a flag waving. Brutus, who has since passed away, was able to experience this paranormal activity before any of us became aware of anything out of the ordinary. Like most animals, he had a keen sense of such things. Brutus was a great field investigator in his own right, and he will be missed.

– Patrick Burke

CHAPTER 18 ~ PHOTOS OF ANOTHER REALM

"You no more win a war than you can win an earthquake."

*- Jeannette Rankin,
former U.S. legislator*

Over the years, we've been fortunate enough to capture a wide variety of paranormal photographs at Gettysburg. Before these "spirit" photos can be analyzed accurately, however, it's important to understand the nature of photography; the history and nature of paranormal photographs; and how to distinguish between genuine paranormal captures and camera glitches, light anomalies or user errors.

One of the most important inventions in history, photography has transformed the way people see the world. With the click of a button, we can capture moments in time and preserve them for years to come. Every so often — at least in theory — we can capture images not seen with the naked eye … images that suggest the existence of paranormal phenomena and defy our understanding of the physical world.

Currently, two technologies make creating photographs possible: traditional film technology and digital imaging technology. Traditional film technology, which dates back almost 200 years, exposes a visual image onto special light-sensitive chemicals within the film. The film contains a physical representation of the image and, once exposed, the transparencies and negatives last for decades. A much newer technology, digital imaging creates a digital representation according to the color and intensity of light falling on an array of special digital receptors. A specialized form of microchip, these sensors measure the amount of light that falls on different parts of the sensor surface in a given time window. The images are digital files stored in digital memory.

People have been capturing ghostly images on film since the early days of photography. Unfortunately, many of the first spirit photos taken in the mid-to-late 1800s were hoaxes, cleverly created by psychic mediums professing to be communicating directly with the dead. Obvious frauds, these photos showed individuals sitting in chairs with the faces of their deceased loved ones hovering in the air around them. Some were even more dubious, showing mediums in supposed trance states spewing ectoplasm (a gauze-like substance associated with the formation of spirits) out of their mouths as they connected with the spirit world.

However, much more compelling photographs — such as the Combermere Abbey ghost taken in 1891, the Brown Lady of Raynham Hall taken in 1936, and the Tulip Staircase ghost taken in 1966 — clearly defy conventional thinking and demand further inquiry. Over the years, thousands of honest and credible people from all walks of life have taken compelling pictures that show various types of paranormal anomalies, including spirit mists and orbs, energy vortexes, and more evidentially convincing apparitional forms, which often show clearly defined facial and body features.

So, can ghostly activity — invisible to the naked eye — be captured on film? Assuming ghosts exist, certain facts regarding human vision and camera mechanics suggest that the answer to this question is "yes." First, let's consider the visible light spectrum. Our eyes are sensitive to light that lies in a very small region of the electromagnetic spectrum known as visible light (which corresponds to a wavelength range of 400-700 nanometers and a color range of violet through red). The human eye isn't capable of seeing radiation within wavelengths outside the visible spectrum. For example, ultraviolet radiation has a shorter wavelength than visible violet light, and infrared radiation has a longer wavelength than visible red light. In traditional film technology, photographic emulsions are more sensitive and can capture wavelengths beyond the visible spectrum. Digital sensors are also sensitive to a range of light wider than we can see. The full, broad spectrum of a film or camera sensor bandwidth can be enhanced even further with the help of various filters and film types. Some researchers theorize that energy patterns of ghosts fall into a spectrum of light that isn't visible to the human eye. If so, it might be possible to capture undetected spirit energy that manifests outside visible wavelengths with either a digital or film camera.

Another variable that may account for the existence of paranormal photographs is shutter speed. Vision is a continuous process of the human eye, but eyelids act as shutters that create a small time gap between two continuous visions. This small time gap is the shutter speed that is adjustable in a camera but natural in the eye. On average, an eye has a shutter speed of around 1/50 of a second. The shutter speed of a camera can be as fast as 1/4000 of a second. If someone fired a gun and the bullet whizzed by, you wouldn't be able to see it, but a camera set at a fast shutter speed could freeze its movement.

The possible nature of spirit might also explain this enigma. Some religious scholars and spiritual practitioners have theorized that spirit energy exists on a higher — and faster — metaphysical plane than humans (who exist on a slower, material plane). If such energy vibrates at an accelerated rate, it might explain why people see shadows or figures moving "out of the corner of their eyes." Theoretically, these fast-moving energy forms can be photographed with the faster shutter speeds associated with camera mechanics.

Another theory suggests that ghosts only make themselves visible when they want to, and that paranormal photographs are "gifts" from the beyond. This may be true, as some researchers believe ghosts absorb energy from their surrounding environments in order to create physical anomalies, including manifesting in the presence of certain individuals. Based on this theory, you could conceivably ask permission of the spirits to allow you to photograph them and hope for the best. Many field investigators have employed this method in an attempt to communicate with these entities.

Over the years, we've captured all types of visual anomalies thanks to the diligent efforts of both our field research team and our weekend investigation guests. The following accounts all have powerful photographic evidence to go along with the eyewitness testimony.

LITTLE ROUND TOP FACE

During the second day of fighting, when Confederate soldiers advanced against the Union army's left flank positioned on Little Round Top, they had to maneuver through the boulders of Devil's Den and across a little stream known as Bloody Run. Members of the Texas and Alabama regiments who managed to make it this far found themselves in a wooded area at the southern base of Little Round Top. It was here that they regrouped and began their uphill assaults against Union Col. Joshua Chamberlain's 20th Maine.

While investigating this area a few years ago, one of the psychics in our group picked up on the presence of a soldier at the base of the hill. We immediately took some EMF readings and registered slightly elevated electromagnetic energy levels. Other team members took photographs of and around the psychic to try and capture any spirit energy that may have been manifesting around her. After about 10 minutes, the readings dissipated and the psychic informed us that the presence was no longer there.

Later that evening, while downloading digital camera files, we noticed an anomaly in one of the photos that was taken at the base of Little Round Top. We zoomed in on the object in question, and when we did, we clearly saw a man's face. Sporting a mustache and hat, he had clearly defined features and

Close-up of a photo that reveals clear features of a man's face, including eyes, nose, jawline, mustache and hat. (Courtesy of Donna Baker)

genuinely looked like a Civil War soldier.

Compelled by the details, we tried to figure out what else it could be by process of elimination. After ruling out glares and other camera glitches, we were left with two possibilities. It was either a genuine paranormal capture or a case of simulacra (an unreal or vague semblance of something).

Supporting the genuine paranormal capture assumption is the fact that the psychic sensitive was picking up on the presence of a soldier at the time the photo was taken, and we also documented elevated electromagnetic energy levels in the area. Simulacra, on the other hand, can be likened to a case of mistaken identity, which occurs because our minds naturally tend to create order out of chaos. In a scenario where trees, bushes, rocks and leaves fill a photograph's frame, people tend to interpret what they see based on what they are more familiar with, such as an animal or a person's face. In reality, the mind is simply trying to put the pieces of a chaotic puzzle together as not to cause confusion. In this particular case, the anomaly stands out clearly. One doesn't have to struggle to create this face in the bushes because it's literally staring right back at you. Another factor that weakens the case for simulacra relates to the corroborative nature of the image and where it was taken. For example, if we had suggested a white tiger was in the photograph, it wouldn't make sense geographically. White tigers are indigenous to Southeast Asia, so why would a ghost of one of these magnificent creatures be captured in Gettysburg unless an old zoo once stood on that spot (which isn't the case). Instead, we clearly see a man's face — replete with mustache and hat — who resembles the prototypical individual who might have died at the base of Little Round Top — a Civil War soldier! Does this confirm a genuine paranormal capture? We can never be completely sure of that, but this photograph definitely represents one of the most persuasive we've ever captured.

DEVIL'S DEN APPARITION

During one of our visits to the battlefield, we were walking among the rocks in Devil's Den when I felt the urge to meander into the wooded area to the south of where the heavy fighting took place. I walked down a small pathway about 200 yards from the big boulders where I felt a profound sense of quiet and stillness. My intuition told me to take photographs of the surrounding area. Nothing of particular interest stuck out in this thicket of trees, yet I felt the need to shoot around 15 frames of film with my Nikon N90 (no flash). I stayed there for about 20 minutes and then caught up with the rest of the group, who were making their way over to the Triangular Field.

When I developed the film, I noticed something strange in one of my photos. I knew immediately that it didn't belong there, and when I looked closer I saw a white figure walking among the trees. Startled, I produced a close-up of the image and knew I had captured something interesting — a figure of a person walking with some type of satchel or small suitcase in one hand. This "individual" also appeared to be wearing a hat and a dress, which made me surmise that it was a woman. The analytical process kicked in as I tried to make sense of the photograph. How did I photograph a female form walking behind Devil's Den? Why is she, or he, carrying a bag? And the obvious question: Why did I capture something that I didn't see with my naked eye?

This photo was taken in the wooded area in Devil's Den. Notice the apparition in the middle.

One of the fun things about ghost hunting is that you get to immerse yourself in history. In fact, the historical context of what you might be experiencing can shed a great deal of light on the phenomenon itself. Nothing (that we know of) happens in a complete vacuum. The philosophical concept of cause and effect still seems to dictate the "who, what, when, where and why" of paranormal activity. By thoroughly studying the history of a haunted location, you can create an accurate road map that can guide you through your investigation and give you a better idea of what you're dealing with.

With this photograph, I knew I needed to find out more information in order to make a better assessment of it. I researched why women might be on the Gettysburg battlefield and was thoroughly enlightened. At night, when the fighting usually subsided, nurses and doctors searched the terrain for wounded soldiers in need of assistance. They usually did this with a lantern and a bag of full of medicines they needed to ease the soldiers' suffering. At Gettysburg, the carnage was so great that wounded men often lay where they fell for days before receiving any help. After the battle was over and the remnants of the two armies left, the townspeople and a small group of doctors and nurses were faced with what must have been a daunting and emotionally draining task — taking care of the dead and wounded. I now had a reference point from which I could objectively quantify the photograph. Women did indeed walk on this battlefield in July 1863, and they would most certainly have been overwhelmed with strong, intense emotions as they performed their grizzly tasks as caregivers amongst some of the greatest carnage ever manifested on American soil.

I also realized that the nature of a haunting can sometimes be more mundane. Gettysburg represents more than just a three-day battle that took place almost 150 years ago. Many generations of individuals lived and died in this area over the course of time without having been privy to the horrors of war. Native Americans also inhabited the area for hundreds of years before Europeans began to settle on the continent. Therefore, from a logical standpoint, the apparitional form in the photograph could be anyone from any number of time periods. However, considering the history of this specific location and the details in the photo, it seems more likely that this could be an energy imprint from the actual battle (or its aftermath).

BALADERRY INN SOLDIERS

The Gettysburg battlefield is dotted with farmhouses, some of which were standing during the time of the battle. In just about every case, these homes were used as either field hospitals to accommodate for the overwhelming amount of wounded men or as headquarters for the highest-ranking officers. Located behind Little Round Top on the eastern edge of the battlefield, the Baladerry Inn was no exception. Now a bed and breakfast, it stood witness to the horrors of July 1863 and still bears the bloodstains on its dining room floor to prove it.

Over the years, we've enjoyed great accommodations and warm hospitality at the Baladerry, whose guests have had their fair share of ghostly encounters. We learned from the proprietor that

Photo taken in the Baladerry. Notice the two male apparitions on the patio outside

people often see soldiers peering through the windows as if they are curious as to what's happening inside. Witnesses have also reported seeing a particularly mischievous soldier who enjoys playfully annoying female patrons. Once, during a meeting we held in the living room, we heard a loud popping sound directly above the head of a young female investigator. Her digital recorder ceased to function, and she became hot and exasperated, as if something, or someone, was purposely encroaching on her personal space.

Late one evening, we were reviewing evidence in the living room while one of our weekend investigation participants took random photographs in the house. After taking a picture from the staircase looking out onto the back deck, she suddenly gasped and said, "Guys, you need to come look at this." We immediately walked over and crowded around her digital camera.

"See outside the French doors, by the lattice?" she asked.

At first, I didn't notice anything because I was looking in the wrong area, but I eventually focused on the right spot and let out a gasp of my own.

"You've got to be kidding me," I said.

Standing outside by the deck were two men dressed in uniforms, looking directly into the living room. They seemed semi-transparent, but we could clearly make out the shapes of their bodies, including heads, necks, torsos and arms. They also appeared to be wearing hats.

"Is anyone outside?" I asked.

We were pretty sure everyone had already gone to bed, but we needed to confirm this. We cautiously ventured out the patio doors and thoroughly checked the entire property, but we found nothing. After downloading the picture onto a computer, we approximated where the figures had been standing when the picture was taken. The next day, we compared the angle of the photo to the deck area and determined that the figures would have been standing in a row of large, thick bushes. This was a problem for several reasons. First, two people couldn't have been standing in that row of bushes because there was absolutely no room to do so. Additionally, the deck was raised, so if the men had actually been standing there, they would have been at least eight feet tall! As with most paranormal photographs, we were left scratching out heads.

Two interesting factors make this photograph worthy of serious discussion. According to the owner of the property, dozens of individuals have reported seeing soldiers looking through the windows, gazing into the house. As such, this represents supportive evidence. Also, their presence fits the historic profile of the property. We didn't capture two people wearing Polo shirts and shorts; we photographed two men wearing what look like uniforms. During the battle, hundreds of soldiers wandered around this property, either because they were wounded, lost or looking for fallen comrades. It is at least plausible, therefore, that we may have photographed the spirits of two of them.

TRIANGULAR FIELD SOLDIERS

Capturing an apparition in a photograph is rare; capturing three of them — all dressed in Army of the Potomac uniforms — simply strains credulity. We've talked about the Triangular Field a great deal in this book, and for good reasons. With so much paranormal activity reported on and around this small patch of land, we tend to spend a great deal of time performing all manner of experiments there.

I love twilight on the battlefield. Also known as "the gloaming," this is the period after sunset before dark when the environment seems surreal. As our eyes adjust to the coming darkness, our surroundings feel different, as if we are teetering on the edge of two separate realities. And so it was on this day, as we attempted to capture some of the anomalies so often described in the Triangular Field.

During this particular investigation, we were fortunate to have a well-reputed psychic medium with us. At dusk, the area was devoid of people, so we thought it might be a good time to follow her into the field and document her reactions. With my camera at my side, I instructed her to start at the fence and walk slowly down to the bottom of the field. Half way down, she stopped in her tracks and told us to take pictures of the area below her by the tree line. As she continued to walk, she picked up on the presence of both Union and Confederate soldiers.

"The air is very heavy here," she observed. "There are men just wandering all around us. It's like nothing I've ever experienced before."

Happy with the results, we finished the experiment and returned to the Baladerry Inn (a.k.a. our base camp), where we began to analyze our video and sound recordings, as well as our photographs. This process is often tedious and unrewarding, but on this night, we were in for a big surprise.

"Were there any reenactors on the field tonight?" asked a team member.

"No, the field was empty. Nobody was there," I responded.

"Well, if that's true, you better come look at this," she said.

What we proceeded to look at was nothing short of astonishing. Beyond the forward glance of the psychic, down by the tree line to her right, were two figures wearing light blue pants and dark blue jackets. They seemed to be either walking or running. To the left of the psychic, we noticed another man down by the edge of the woods. Sitting on a rock or tree stump, he was wearing light blue pants and a dark blue jacket, as well as a dark blue kepi. We hadn't seen these men in the field, and there's no way we could've missed them, so where did they come from?

Capturing the spirit forms of three Union soldiers in one photograph seems unbelievable, yet there they are, doing whatever soldiers do when wandering around the place where they probably met their demise. Did the camera catch a glimpse of the actual battle, which manifested at that particular moment due to residual energies still present — yet not visible to the naked eye — on the field of battle?

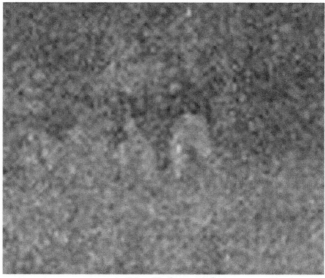

Un-Enhanced

Enhanced

It's very difficult to verify anomalous photographs as proof of the existence of ghostly phenomena — whether genuine, residual or otherwise. On the other hand, we can't simply dismiss all of these photographs as camera glitches or user error because they often show clear, identifiable images that corroborate unexplained activity that occurs in those specific locations. In the examples above, we feel these images represent strong evidence in favor of the presence of either spirit or residual energies. We'll probably never know for sure if these pictures have revealed a glimpse into the spiritual realm, but we owe it to ourselves to consider all possibilities.

— Jack Roth

CHAPTER 19 - THE MISSISSIPPI BOYS JOIN IN

"I believe in the immortality of the soul because I have within me immortal longings."

- Helen Keller

It was late in September 2004 when my team was asked to take a group of investigators to Gettysburg. They wanted to see some hot spots where we had experienced paranormal phenomena on previous investigations. I took a small group to the Copse of Trees on Cemetery Ridge, just behind the stone wall where Confederate Gen. Lewis Armistead crossed over during Trimble/Pickett's Charge. After I was done with this guided walkthrough, I decided to visit the site of the William Bliss Farmhouse and Barn, which stood in the no-man's land between the Confederate forces on

General Pickett

Seminary Ridge and the Union Army on Cemetery Ridge. The Bliss Farm was the subject of fierce fighting on both the second and third days of the battle and was the perfect place for sharpshooters on both sides to harass their enemy. It was also the site of a great controversy.

I wanted to get a head start, so I told the group I would meet them at the Bliss Farm. At approximately 9 p.m. I began my short drive to Seminary Ridge. The night was cool and I could see my breath in the chilly air. A scattering of clouds danced with the moon. I pulled over to the side of the road near where Confederate Gen. Carnot Posey's Mississippi Brigade started their attack on July 2, 1863. I turned off the car lights and stepped into the pitch black of night. I stood there for several minutes acclimating to the night sounds and let my eyes adjust to the darkness. I felt as if I was being watched, which is something I've experienced many times before during battlefield investigations. I quietly said "hello" and poured some water for any thirsty souls who might be present.

I crossed the road towards the open fields of the Bliss Farm and wondered what it must have been like for Posey and his men during the battle. Posey's brigade was composed of four Mississippi regiments of infantry, and formed part of Gen. Richard Anderson's division of Gen. A.P. Hill's Third Corps. The brigade assisted in the attack against the Union positions along Cemetery Ridge and towards the heights of Little Round Top and the Devil's Den on July 2.

On that day, a Union skirmish line held the Bliss Farmhouse and Barn, but Posey's brigade attacked and took hold of the buildings for a short time until Union reinforcements forced them to retreat. The Mississippians reformed and drove the Union troopers out of the farmhouse and barn, but instead of advancing and supporting Gen. Ambrose Wright's Georgia Brigade on their right, they stayed and held the buildings. The controversy as to whether Posey had orders to hold his position or advance to Cemetery Ridge and help Wright remains unsettled today.

In The War of the Rebellion: A Compilation of the Official Records of the Union and Confederate Armies, Wright reported:

"We were now within less than 100 yards of the crest of the heights, which were lined with artillery, supported by a strong line of infantry,

under protection from a stone fence. My men, by a well-directed fire, soon drove the cannoneers from their guns, and, leaping over the fence, charged up the top of the crest, and drove the enemy's infantry into a rocky gorge on the eastern slope of the heights, and some 80 or 100 yards in rear of the enemy's batteries. We were now complete masters of the field, having gained the key, as it were, of the enemy's whole line."

Wright could have maintained the heights on Cemetery Ridge, changing the complexity of the battle dramatically, but through some strange twist of fate he wasn't supported in his advance. He continued in his report:

"Unfortunately, just as we had carried the enemy's last and strongest position, it was discovered that the brigade on our right had not only not advanced across the turnpike, but had actually given way, and was rapidly falling back to the rear, while on our left we were entirely unprotected, the brigade ordered to our support having failed to advance ... I have not the slightest doubt but that I should have been able to have maintained my position on the heights, and secured the captured artillery, if there had been a protecting force on my left, or if the brigade on my right had not been forced to retire."

Perception is relative. From the point of view of Wright, he was let down by Posey and other Confederate forces. But what about Posey's perception of the facts? If he did, in fact, receive orders to hold the Bliss Farm, he would have obeyed those orders and felt an immense amount of pride in doing so. Although Posey did send several regiments forward at different times, he never advanced in force, which was the original concept and plan that Lee put forth. One of Posey's regiments, the 19th Mississippi, did advance forward with Wright's Brigade all the way to Brian's Barn, but they were told by an officer to fall back, not once, but three times.

Unfortunately, conflicting recollections and the passage of time have clouded what happened on that day. Some historians, and the people who read specific accounts like Wright's above, will always believe that Posey's brigade somehow failed in their duty, which isn't fair to the brave Mississippians who fought so hard to secure this strategic patch of land.

After I offered up some water to the thirsty troops, I stepped over the rock wall and into the open field towards the Bliss Farm. Suddenly, the feeling of extreme hunger struck me. "Odd," I thought to myself. "I just ate a satisfying meal at the Lincoln Diner." Could I be having an interactive experience with one of Posey's men?

I entered the field just as the moon broke through some clouds and bathed the field in front of me in moonlight. "Well boys," I said aloud in a southern drawl, "I'll be stepping off now to the farm ahead; you can join me if you've a mind to." As soon as I started walking, a rush of energy hit me violently — apprehension, anticipation, fear and determination all mingled together in a tidal wave of emotion.

This makes a person wonder how they might react in a battlefield situation. I began to pick up my pace, feeling the need to gain the cover of the farmhouse as quickly as possible. Off to my right I heard several men walking; seconds later, the same sounds came from my left. Was this a residual haunting or a genuine, live interaction? Ghosts react to our energy, and there are many times when we walk into a room or area and set off a genuine haunting experience. It was almost 800 yards to the remains of the Bliss farmhouse and another 200 yards to where the barn used to be. The ghost soldiers continued to walk with me until I saw the LED flashlight of one of my team members pointed in my direction. Before I headed back towards the group, I stopped and said thank you to the Mississippi boys for their company and bid them farewell.

I can only wonder if some of the fallen soldiers from Posey's brigade still walk the fields in and around the Bliss Farm area, waiting to be vindicated from any controversies related to their actions on July 2, 1863, when the chaos and confusion of battle often prevailed over objective thinking.

– Patrick Burke

CHAPTER 20 ~ THE ETERNAL BATTLE

"My dead and wounded were nearly as great in number as those still on duty. They literally covered the ground. The blood stood in puddles in some places on the rocks; the ground was soaked with the blood of as brave men as ever fell on the red field of battle."

- Colonel William C. Oates, 15th Alabama, at Little Round Top

A view from Little Roun Top looking down into The Valley of Death.

Nestled on the crest of the southern slope of Little Round Top, the patch of ground where Union Col. Joshua Lawrence Chamberlain and the 20th Maine repulsed Confederate attempts to collapse the

Union left flank appears inconspicuous enough. In fact, when we attempted to find this location during our first ever visit to the battlefield, we struggled to find it. Once we did, paranormal activity began in earnest before we could even unpack any of our equipment.

We arrived at the battlefield on a beautiful fall afternoon, drove around and eventually headed towards the two rocky hills that marked the locations of Little Round Top and Big Round Top. Winding roads lined with memorials guided us around the Valley of Death and Devil's Den and finally to the base of Little Round Top.

As we drove, we felt overwhelmed by the significance of the location. We were in Gettysburg, where for three days in 1863 some of the most vicious and costly fighting ever experienced by armies took place on American soil; where more than 51,000 casualties accumulated like snow flakes during a winter storm as armed men fought to the death over political and moral issues that many of them didn't bother to comprehend. The events that played out on this patch of land signified the turning point of the Civil War, which on a larger scale was a critical turning point in the

View from the Visitor's Tour at Little Round Top's summit.

history of our young nation. Before 9/11, everything we knew about this country could be categorized in terms of "before the Civil War" and "after the Civil War." We were in arguably the most significant place in U.S. history, where tens of thousands of young men experienced the hellish and indescribable nature of warfare.

The summit of Little Round Top — like the rest of the battlefield — is strewn with monuments dedicated to various individuals, companies, regiments, and corps. The fighting on and around Little Round Top on July 2, 1863 was both intense and strategically critical. Union Gen. Strong Vincent's brigade held off wave after relentless wave of Confederate assaults as a number of Alabama and Texas regiments from Maj. Gen. John Bell Hood's division attempted to flank the Army of the Potomac. Chamberlain's 20th Maine successfully defended the end of the Union line on the southern slope (the extreme left), with the engagement culminating in a dramatic downhill bayonet charge that essentially ended the Southern advance.

The significance of this action cannot be overstated: If Chamberlain and his men had faltered that day, Southern forces would have flanked the Union left and crushed the Federal army in a rout. Instead, the failure to break the Union's defensive line forced Gen. Lee into attempting an ill-advised assault (Pickett's Charge) on the Union center the following day, which led to a devastating Southern defeat and the end of the Battle of Gettysburg. Many historians believe it also marked the beginning of the end for the Confederacy.

Thirty years later, Chamberlain received a Congressional Medal of Honor for his conduct in the defense of Little Round Top. The citation read that he was awarded for "daring heroism and great tenacity in holding his position on the Little Round Top against repeated assaults, and carrying the advance position on the Great Round Top." Col. William C. Oates of the 15th Alabama, who lost his brother John during those series of charges, strongly believed that if his regiment had been able to take Little Round Top, the Army of Northern Virginia might have won the battle, and possibly marched on to take Washington, D.C. He concluded philosophically that:

"His [Chamberlain's] skill and persistency and the great bravery of his men saved Little Round Top and the Army of the Potomac from defeat ... great events sometimes turn on comparatively small affairs."

We finally came upon a small plaque that directed us to the spot where Chamberlain formed his defensive line, and we slowly made our way down a narrow path to the remnants of a line of earthworks. We couldn't help but feel a profound sense of respect as we stood in the footsteps of hundreds of brave soldiers who never made it off Little Round Top alive.

Instinctively, we began to canvas the area. My fellow investigator, Sean, immediately headed down the slope on which Confederate forces had relentlessly attempted their uphill attack. As darkness began to fall, I found myself sitting on a rock along the Union line, contemplating what it must have been like to be one of Chamberlain's men, facing a continuous onslaught of bullets, when the following dialogue ensued:

Sean (annoyed): Very funny, guys!

Jack: What?

Sean: Was that you, Scott?

There was no answer, as Scott had walked back down the path towards the viewing station at the summit of the hill. Obviously, Sean believed Scott was trying to scare him.

Sean (more annoyed): That's just not cool.

Jack: Sean, Scott's not here, and I'm sitting about 20 yards above you on a rock along where the Union defensive line formed. What happened?

Sean (now in a state of obvious excitement): Are you serious? Somebody just walked right passed me and breezed by my left side. I saw a guy walk right towards me and I thought it was Scott. It had to be Scott.

Jack: I'm coming down there. Don't move.

I moved quickly down the hill.

As I hurried toward Sean, I heard the shuffling of leaves to my left, as if someone was scurrying along beside me … and then I heard rustling to my right. I stopped a few feet from Sean, becoming very still and observant. Sean stood frozen, as if paralyzed by some type of ray gun.

Jack: Did you hear that?"

Sean: Yes ... loud and clear. What the hell was that?

Jack: I have no idea. What did you see?

I listened for more footfalls on the slope, but heard nothing.

Sean: I was walking along slowly, trying to get a feel for what it must have looked like to the Confederates attacking uphill, when suddenly I saw the shadowy figure of a man — who at the time I thought was Scott — walking from that tree [points to his right] towards me. I turned back around and suddenly felt as if somebody brushed up beside me, but there was nobody there. That's when I assumed Scott was trying to rattle me."

Jack: Can you describe the figure?

Sean: The man looked to be about 5'8", thin and I could have sworn he was wearing a cap on his head. Not like a cowboy hat or baseball cap, but more like a kepi or bummer. I couldn't make out a uniform, just the outline of the body and the small cap on his head. He was moving from right to left if you were watching from the bottom of the hill, and he was moving pretty fast.

Jack: You felt him brush by you?"

Sean: Yes, like a breeze, but definitely a tangible feeling of somebody whisking by me. There was a real sense of urgency with this guy, like he was trying to get somewhere fast.

Jack: Frantic, like during a battle maybe?

Sean: Exactly. Like he was running for his life, but I feel like my movements precipitated his movements, if that makes sense.

Jack: I know what you mean, because when I rushed down the slope to get to you, we heard the shuffling on either side of me, like others were running alongside me.

We stood for a few minutes, listening for any sounds and straining to see in the low-light conditions. It soon became too dark, and we didn't have any equipment with us, so we decided to call it a night and check into our bed and breakfast. As we walked back up the hill, we saw Scott walking down the path towards us.

Scott: This place is amazing. You can see a good portion of the battlefield from that viewing tower. Anything interesting happen here?

Sean (smiling): You have no idea.

*Dead soldiers from both armies were strewn all over
Little Round Top.*

As we left the battlefield, I wondered if the spirits of the soldiers who died there could react to our actions as if the battle was still in progress. If we made any sudden movements, for example, would they instinctually — as a result of having become emotionally attached to the location — spring into action, fighting on that hill as if it was still a hot afternoon in July 1863?

In order to understand how phenomena like this can occur, we must first examine a few of the basic laws of biology and thermodynamics. First and foremost, the fact that everything in the universe is energy has significant relevance as it applies to the possible existence of ghosts. Science has confirmed that energy exists everywhere and when in motion creates an energy field allowing energy to be absorbed, conducted and transmitted. Our bodies radiate, absorb and conduct frequency waves of energy, and each of our senses works through energies at specific frequency bands along the electromagnetic spectrum. Most surprisingly, if we magnify the cells, molecules and atoms of which we're composed, we can see that at the most basic level we're made up of subtle energy fields containing little, if any, matter. We aren't merely physical and chemical structures, but beings composed of energy.

As such, let's look at the first law of thermodynamics, which is an expression of the principle of conservation of energy that states that energy can be transformed (changed from one form to another), but cannot be created or destroyed. Based on these principles, we can now make an educated assumption that a transformation — not the destruction — of energy occurs at the time of physical death. At this point the second law of thermodynamics takes effect. This law states that energy is dispersed from a core source and radiates outward in a symmetrical pattern until "acted upon." This happens as a consequence of the assumed randomness of molecular chaos, and it's also where the final pieces of the puzzle in regards to the creation of ghosts remain unidentified.

The second law dictates that upon death of the physical body human energies generally disperse in a natural manner. Does this suggest that fragments of our conscious (or subconscious) thought can — at least for a while —interact with the surrounding environment in which bodily death occurred? What if this energy is "acted upon" in a way that either slows down or stops dispersal altogether? Can a traumatic death, for example, create a "shockwave" that affects energy in such a way as to bind it to a specific time and place?

If you consider ghostly behavior, it makes sense. For the most part, haunting phenomena tend to be fragmented in nature. You hear footsteps, see a shadow out of the corner of your eye or hear a disembodied voice calling out your name ... but whatever transpires only lasts momentarily. When sentient behavior manifests, it's as if the ghost is suffering from dementia or some stage of Alzheimer's disease. They exist in a haze, as if coherent thought is difficult. When you capture EVP, it's usually a sound, a word or two, or in rare instances a short sentence. Examples of EVP we've captured over the years include "cold," "mommy," a giggle, the rebel yell, a bouncing ball and a gunshot. The most complete sentence we've ever captured was, "Won't you help me?" and the most compelling EVP I've ever heard from Gettysburg was, "I knew George Pickett." Truly profound, but only four words, not exactly the Gettysburg Address.

The bouncing ball and the gunshot can be categorized as residual in nature, but when a form of consciousness seems to be present and interaction of some kind occurs, we're left with more questions than answers. As it applies to what happened to us on Little Round Top, we can see how the scientific laws mentioned above might corroborate the existence of the shadowy figure and the rustling of the leaves on the ground.

Here's one explanation of what happened: On July 2, 1863, soldiers die on Little Round Top. Their deaths are traumatic in every sense of the word. When their physical bodies expire, their energy fields survive and transform, dispersing in a random way into the environment. Because of the emotional and sudden nature of the transformation, the last conscious thought gets stuck, thus remaining in the moment it was created just before bodily death. More than 14 decades later, we arrive at Little Round Top and start walking around. One of these fragments of consciousness recognizes — on a purely instinctive and reactionary level — a man (Sean) walking down the slope of the hill. This particular energy field springs into action as if the battle is still raging, brushing past Sean as either a comrade in arms or mortal enemy. Sean sees the shadowy figure of a man and feels him brush by his shoulder, but then the event stops. Sean calls out, and I start walking down the hill towards him. Other energy fields present on the hill also react, following me down as if participating in Chamberlain's counterattack. I hear the rustling of leaves and twigs around me as I head down the hill. When I reach Sean, the ruckus around us stops. The paranormal event ends, and we leave the area having had our first paranormal experience at Gettysburg.

So what happened? Is it plausible that fragmented thought forms — which once existed in whole form as living, breathing human beings — still wander about the battlefield, reacting to their surroundings in a purely random and chaotic manner? This is but a theory, but a theory based in some part on accepted scientific laws. By simply continuing along a line of logic, you can easily come to the conclusion that, at the very least, consciousness survives death. What happens to us when we die can be debated, but the fact that we continue on in some form appears obvious to those who experience such events.

— Jack Roth

Jack with reenactors.

CHAPTER 21 ~ FIELD INVESTIGATION TIPS

"Thus ended the great American Civil War,
which upon the whole must be considered
the noblest and least avoidable of all the great
mass conflicts of which till then there was record."

-Winston Churchill,
A History of the English-Speaking Peoples

Throughout this book, we have documented first-hand accounts and photographic evidence, and discussed theoretical possibilities pertaining to paranormal phenomena experienced in and around Gettysburg and its historic battlefield. We hope you have learned a thing or two about this mysterious and beautiful place, and we also encourage you to get out there and go to haunted locations to perform well-executed investigations that will yield viable results for the good of the entire research community.

Having said this, paranormal field investigators should remain cognizant of the following when investigating haunted locations such as Gettysburg:

- Keep an open mind regarding quantum theory and the general laws of physics. You don't have to be a physicist to be a good paranormal investigator, but you should read the equivalent of Quantum Physics 101 in order to gain a basic understanding of the physical laws of the universe and how they might relate to paranormal phenomena.

- Bring a broad array of environmental measuring tools, including geomagnetic field meters, electromagnetic field meters, temperature gauges, humidity gauges, barometric pressure gauges, radiometers, ion detectors, etc. These tools will help you document baseline readings and record any anomalous deviations from those baseline readings.

- Document every small detail of the landscape in question. Note the topography including rock types and formations (Devil's Den), and take latitude, longitude and elevation readings (Little Round Top) to create an accurate grid of the area being investigated. These topographical details might play a role in triggering the phenomena. Be sure to document by taking plenty of still photographs.

- Research as many cases regarding residual hauntings as possible in order to create a model on which to build an investigative strategy. For example, many imprint hauntings are preceded by a palpable change in atmosphere. By knowing what to look — and feel — for, you can be prepared when environmental fluctuations occur.

- Understand that consciousness plays a factor in these phenomena; therefore, it's important to utilize a good medium and/or sensitive during field investigations in order to localize paranormal energies and document the effects these environments have on certain individuals.

- Interview eyewitnesses beforehand in order to determine optimal focus areas. For example, many incidents at Gettysburg that fit the profile for imprint hauntings occur in the Triangular Field. Knowing this, you should focus on conducting particular experiments and taking specific readings in this area. Compiling large documentation at a specific location can be beneficial to future research.

- Ask experts in particular disciplines for ideas on what they might want documented at a particular location or investigation. By doing so, you can accumulate data potentially beneficial to other researchers moving forward. It will also help you develop strong investigative techniques and protocols, and you will end up with solid research as a result.

- Make sure you have a well-balanced team. Your field investigation team should include a team leader, whose job it is to make sure the team stays on task and has the historical research on hand to help direct the investigation; a sensitive; an equipment/tech person; a photographer; and a documenter, whose job it is to take copious notes and collect all of the field data. We also suggest bringing along a second sensitive; the two of them can help validate and enhance the information being obtained by one another.

- Share your research with others! In order to make progress in any area of study, a clearinghouse of information must be made available to all researchers. The sharing of thoughts and ideas is the fastest way to enlightenment.

In the end, all we can do as paranormal field researchers is use our investigative skills, our intuition and the proper equipment to best obtain and document a body of evidence that may someday assist physicists, psychologists and other scientists as they attempt to answer life's most profound questions. Gettysburg provides the perfect "outdoor laboratory" in which to do this.

The Civil War-era American poet Nathaniel Hawthorne once wrote:

"Our Creator would never have made such lovely days and have given us the deep hearts to enjoy them, above and beyond all thought, unless we were meant to be immortal."

We believe, as did Hawthorne, that human beings are innately aware of something metaphysical, something highly abstract that exists beyond the physical world (in which we only exist temporarily).

Humanity's quest for knowledge underscores this awareness. As it applies to paranormal research on battlefields, we owe it to ourselves and the millions of ghost soldiers around the world to optimize the knowledge that can be gleaned from the etchings of their heroic sacrifices, respect those sacrifices, and enjoy the journey of exploration along the way.

— Jack Roth and Patrick Burke

AFTERWORD

Control.

It's a word scientist's love, and an environment they demand when conducting research. Laboratories offer the most controlled environments, as parapsychologist and paranormal research pioneer J.B. Rhine and his team proved when they conducted successful extrasensory perception (ESP) experiments at Duke University in the 1920s and 1930s. Rhine's experimentation led to reliable analysis due to the replication of his observations. To this day ESP is the only paranormal occurrence to which some scientists will acquiesce, in large part due to Rhine's efforts.

Unfortunately, most paranormal phenomena dictate that researchers and investigators leave the comfortable confines of the laboratory and venture out into the field. This, after all, is where the action is. A wise man once said that if you want to catch fish, go where the fish are. The same principle applies to ghosts, as only so much can be gleaned about ghostly phenomena in a laboratory.

The problem: Too many unknown variables taint evidence, rendering it useless to those who subscribe to the scientific method. The scientific method demands observation, hypothesis, experimentation, analysis, conclusion and theory. In the field, it's often difficult to cover the stages of scientific rigor in the few seconds an anomaly might occur, and you can't go back and make it happen again on demand (lack of repeatability). Spirits don't keep schedules, and emotional imprints can't be bottled up for laboratory analysis, at least not yet.

Having said this, some of the most active — and challenging — places on which to conduct paranormal research are battlefields. These historic landmarks have presented difficult challenges to field researchers. Some of these hindrances include natural elements associated with the outdoors such as rain, wind and extreme temperatures, which all can affect electronic equipment, film stock and an investigator's fortitude. Indigenous animals can make it difficult to conduct electronic voice phenomena (EVP) experiments, as the sounds they make can be easily misinterpreted as paranormal in nature.

And then there are people. Millions of tourists visit battlefields every year. During the course of any given day, hundreds of school buses drop off children of all ages to explore these hallowed grounds. At Gettysburg, some of these kids tend to run around Devil's Den like it's a Chuck E. Cheese's. It's important that children experience these places, but it's a nightmare for field researchers!

Large battlefields such as Gettysburg cover more than 10 square miles, and strange anomalies have been experienced on just about every portion of it. Remember, the larger the area in which you conduct an experiment, the less control you have over outside elements. Lugging around hundreds of pounds of equipment over long distances is no walk in the park. Storing equipment, keeping it safe, and having appropriate power sources in the middle of a battlefield can be a tricky proposition when the nearest shelter or power source is hundreds of yards, or even miles, away.

Topography also adds to the chaos. Battlefields are covered with trees, bushes, logs, leaves and rocks — a perfect environment in which to see a thousand faces on Mars! Remember, the mind creates familiarity out of chaos (simulacra), so in a place like Gettysburg, every photograph can conceivably have a blurry tree or moss-covered rock in the background that will look like a soldier once the mind connects the dots.

Adding to these headaches are time and money. Some battlefield parks have bank hours, so your time may be limited once it gets dark. Unless you want to spend time in county lock up, you need to take the time to secure the appropriate permits, or permission, depending on where you go. Also, traveling costs money, whether you travel by car (gas), airplane (ticket expenses) or horse and buggy (time away from work!). Field investigators traverse long distances in order to "go where the fish are." Such research can be likened to expeditions that require planning and smart logistical execution.

Although these obstacles can be daunting, there are things you can do to make your battlefield investigation a success. For example, always pick smaller areas in which to conduct experiments. Remember, you have more control the smaller your "outdoor laboratory." In Gettysburg, we narrow our experiments to specific parts of the battlefield. On the 26-acre Wheatfield, for example, we conduct a grid-like walkthrough with several participants. These investigators walk across the field at 20 yards apart holding handheld equipment such as cameras, tape recorders and TriField Meters. Simultaneously, we set up video cameras on higher elevations that offer wide-angle views of the entire field. The result — several people with possible psi abilities being documented exploring every inch of the field while holding environmental monitoring equipment.

As mentioned above, battlefields are covered with trees, bushes, tall grass, dead logs and rocks. At various angles, these objects can look like soldiers, horses and other battlefield objects. In order to document locations properly, always shoot a series of photos to create a panoramic view of the entire area from where you stand. By doing so, you cover every angle and can better determine if that bearded Union soldier is actually a jagged rock with fungus and moss growing on it. Another effective way to decrease the chances of misinterpretation is by setting up a triangulated coverage with video equipment. Triangulation is an approach to data analysis that synthesizes data from multiple sources. By having multiple video sources in which to view various angles of Devil's Den, for example, we can rule out a false positive by viewing the ghostly image from another angle and determining its only a rock that happens to looks like a man's face from one particular angle. Triangulation can also help corroborate something as being paranormal in nature if more than one camera picks up the same anomaly.

In the end, field investigations are imperative to paranormal research. Rhine proved certain phenomena could be observed and replicated in a laboratory. Some of the more unpredictable phenomena, however, cannot. Therefore, interaction with the environments where these events occur is necessary. Environmental factors that are geographically specific such as electromagnetic field anomalies, family dynamics and traumatic historical events seem to play a role in various types of hauntings, so being in the trenches can yield the best evidence as it applies to the affects of these variables. Importantly, interviewing eyewitnesses where the phenomena occur — not in a parapsychologist's office or laboratory — seems to be the best way to extract accurate testimony due to familiar triggers in the environment.

As field researchers, we can put forth due diligence in order to gather acceptable evidence, especially if, over long periods of time, we can establish trends that give scientists something with which to attempt to replicate either in the field or in a laboratory.

We intend for this book to be the first in a collaborative series that documents compelling evidence collected on battlefields across the world. Our goal is to accumulate a body of evidence that compels other researchers and scientists to recognize the importance of battlefields as they apply to paranormal research.

Life happens "out there," and that's where we need to be in order to find the elusive answers to life's most puzzling enigmas. Our experiences at Gettysburg have taught us that exploring the unknown represents an unparalleled adventure and that investigating battlefields results in a clearer understanding of both historical events and the specific sacrifices associated with war that make them such horrific, yet enduring, of all human experiences.

— Jack and Patrick

ABOUT THE AUTHORS

JACK ROTH - Jack's strong interest in photography is what initially led him to the world of the paranormal. While examining photographs he took at the Myrtles Plantation (La.) in 1995, he noticed some strange anomalies. It was after this event that Jack decided to use his journalism and writing skills to pursue paranormal research.In 1997, he wrote and co produced a TV demo titled Hauntings: A Journey Into the Unknown. Due to the profound and life-changing nature of the experiences he had during that project, he realized that both the scientific and spiritual implications of paranormal phenomena needed to be considered seriously. Jack appeared as a principle investigator in Ghost Detectives, a one-hour TV special produced in 2001 that continues to air on the Discovery Channel. In 2007, he was interviewed for the Gettysburg-based documentary titled The Other Side: Giving Up the Ghost. Most recently, he has participated as an on-camera paranormal investigator in several TV demos for the Emmy Award-winning production company Lightworks-KPI Productions. Jack and noted paranormal investigator Patrick Burke (American Battlefield Ghost Hunters Society and Trent Hall Media Group) recently completed their first collaborative book effort, Ghost Soldiers™ of Gettysburg, and have begun work on their second title in the series, Ghost Soldier of Antietam.

PATRICK BURKE - Patrick has been an investigator and teacher in the paranormal field for over 30 years. He is a self-taught military historian with the gift of psychic sensitivity. This perfect match of ability and interest has created a skilled and knowledgeable investigator. His natural aptitude for leadership has helped him teach others, both in the field and in the classroom. Patrick has made appearances on The Michael Medved Show, Joshua Warren's Weird or What, International Paranormal Investigators Radio, and Ghostly Talk Radio. He has given lectures at HorrorFind, ABGHS's Boot Camp, George Mason University Book Fair, and Washington College. His reputation as the authority on battlefield ghost hunting is internationally known. His first book, Battlefield Guide to Ghost Hunting, is currently available. Patrick and paranormal researcher Jack Roth recently completed their first collaborative book effort, Ghost Soldiers™ of Gettysburg, and have begun work on their second title in the series, Ghost Soldiers™ of Antietam.Patrick's famed American Battlefield Ghost Hunters Society has grown and developed into Trent Hall Media Group, www.trenthallmedia.com. Additionally, he is working with Emmy Award-winning production company Lightworks-KPI Productions and world-renown paranormal researcher and author, Joshua Warren, on several projects.

CPSIA information can be obtained at www.ICGtesting.com
Printed in the USA
LVOW040300161211

259558LV00002B/234/P